Contents

To the student

A close reading of the play is the student's primary task, but it is well worth seeing a performance if possible. These Notes will help to increase your understanding and appreciation of the play, and to stimulate *your own* thinking about it: *they are in no way intended as a substitute* for a thorough knowledge of the play.

Norman T. Carrington MA

Brodie's Notes on Shakespeare's

The Winter's Tale

Pan Books London and Sydney

First published 1977 by Pan Books Ltd,
Cavaye Place, London SW10 9PG
2 3 4 5 6 7 8 9
All rights reserved
© James Brodie Ltd 1977
ISBN 0 330 50100 3
Printed and bound in Great Britain by
Richard Clay (The Chaucer Press) Ltd, Bungay, Suffolk

The author and his work

Surprisingly little is known of the life of our greatest dramatist, and the little we can be sure about comes mainly from
brief references to him in legal or other formal documents.
Though there is no record of Shakespeare's actual birth date,
we do know that he was christened William at the market
town of Stratford-on-Avon on 26 April 1564. He was the
third child of John Shakespeare – variously described as
glover, wool dealer, farmer and butcher – and Mary Arden,
whose family were prosperous local landowners. However,
until the year 1578, when his business began to decline, John
Shakespeare was a notable figure in Stratford, and William was
probably educated at the local grammar school – where
he would have learned the 'small Latin and less Greek' of
which the playwright Ben Jonson (1572–1637) accused him.
But John Aubrey (1626–97) in his *Brief Lives* (written in the
seventeenth century but not published until 1813) says that
Shakespeare had 'enough education to become a school-
master' – and stated categorically that his father was *not* a
butcher.

In 1582, at the age of eighteen, Shakespeare married
Anne Hathaway, a woman eight years his senior, who bore
him two girls and a boy: Susanna in 1583 and the twins
Hamnet and Judith in 1585. He is thought to have left Stratford for London in 1585: there is a tradition (which Aubrey
does not deny) that Shakespeare had to flee his native town
to avoid prosecution for stealing deer in Sir Thomas Lucy's
grounds. But, more to the point, it seems that he left with a
band of strolling players, the Queen's Players, who visited
Stratford in 1585.

Whether he took his wife and children with him to
London is not known, but a pamphlet published in 1592 by

a lesser playwright Robert Greene mentions Shakespeare as an actor and playwright. Plague caused the theatres to close in 1593; on their reopening in the following year we know that Shakespeare was by then a member of The Lord Chamberlain's Company (known after the accession of James I as The King's Men). It is probable that he stayed with this company throughout the remainder of his career, writing plays and acting in them in various theatres. His connection with the company must have brought him considerable financial reward, and Shakespeare seems to have been a good businessman as well, for when he retired to Stratford in 1611, aged forty-seven, he was already a fairly wealthy man and a shareholder in two theatres, the Globe and the Blackfriars. He purchased New Place, one of the largest houses in Stratford – where he entertained Ben Jonson and the poet Michael Drayton (1563–1631), and – by the astute purchase of tithes and arable land – he became, in the tradition of his maternal forefathers, a prosperous landowner. He died in Stratford-on-Avon on 23 April 1616, survived by his wife and two daughters.

As an actor Shakespeare does not seem to have been particularly successful; but even in his own day his fame as a dramatist and his personal popularity were great. In 1598 Francis Meres (1567–1647), the writer of critical assessments of playwrights, described Shakespeare as 'the most excellent in both kinds' [i.e. in comedy and in tragedy], and even Ben Jonson, whose dramatic work was in a very different vein, remarks of Shakespeare in *Discoveries* (published posthumously in 1640), 'I lov'd the man and do honour his memory (on this side idolatry) as much as any.' And John Milton (1608–74) wrote in his poem 'l'Allegro' (1632) the often-quoted lines: 'Or sweetest Shakespeare fancy's child/ Warble his native woodnotes wild.'

Shakespeare probably began his work as a dramatist by collaborating with others and patching up old plays for his company to revive. His first completely original play is believed to be *Love's Labour's Lost* (?1590), though the date of each play presents a problem: the dates are not given in the First Folio (the first collected edition of his plays, 1632). His first narrative poems, composed during the Plague when the theatres were closed, were *Venus and Adonis* (1593) and *The Rape of Lucrece* (1594). His 154 *Sonnets* were published in 1609 – without Shakespeare's permission, it is said. The first 126 of these intensely personal poems are addressed to a young man, the poet's friend and patron; the remainder to a 'dark lady'. The identity of neither of these two inspirers of the sonnets has been established – nor has it been decided how far the series is autobiographical.

Most of the plays were written for performance in the public playhouses, and were conveniently classified in the First Folio in three groups: comedies, histories and tragedies. But these divisions are too arbitrary – the 'comedies' can contain tragedy, the 'tragedies' moments of mirth, and the 'histories' have aspects of both tragedy and comedy.

When, however, the plays are considered chronologically they fall naturally into four periods. From about **1590–93** Shakespeare was **learning his trade** while patching up existing plays and beginning to write his own: to this period belong *Love's Labour's Lost*, *The Comedy of Errors*, *Two Gentlemen of Verona*, the three *Parts* of *Henry VI*, *Romeo and Juliet* and *Richard III.*

From about **1594–1600** was the period of Shakespeare's **greatest development**, when he wrote such plays as *Titus Andronicus*, *A Midsummer Night's Dream*, *The Merchant of Venice*, *The Taming of the Shrew*, the two *Parts* of *Henry IV*, *The Merry Wives of Windsor*, *As You Like It* and *Twelfth Night*.

Despite what we have said above, the period between **1602–08** can be described as that of *the tragedies*, which include *Hamlet*, *Othello*, *King Lear*, *Macbeth* and *Antony and Cleopatra*.

Shakespeare's **final period (1610–13)** includes three romances: *The Tempest*, *Cymbeline* and *The Winter's Tale*; and one historical play, *Henry VIII*.

As for the original production of these plays, Shakespeare cared little about the dress of his characters – irrespective of place or period, the actors wore the English fashions of his time. And, whatever might be a play's geographical setting, his clowns and lower-class characters were true London cockneys or British country bumpkins – such as would appeal to the gallery in English playhouses.

Since that time, there have been many fashions in 'dressing' the plays: there have been attempts at contemporaneous setting and clothes – in more recent times some of the plays have been produced against stark backgrounds and in modern dress. But today there is a movement towards vaguely 'historical' dress, and (after decades of sonorous, sometimes pompous and often unintelligible speaking of the lines) to a simpler, more naturalistic delivery, such as Shakespeare's original players probably used. But, notwithstanding the many and various innovations over the years, Shakespeare's genius, his lyrical lines and wonderful choice of words, his warmth and his understanding of the human predicament, continue to bring entertainment and enlightenment to people all over the world.

The Elizabethan Theatre

At the time of Shakespeare there were probably not more than five public theatres in the land, all in London, and they were built according to the design of the inn-yards of the period, which had been found marvellously convenient places for the presentation of plays.

The theatre was circular or octagonal in shape. The main part of the auditorium was the large round pit, open to the sky, in which the poorer people *stood* (the 'groundlings'). Encircling this, round the walls, were three balconies, covered on top but not in front (like the 'stands' on a football ground), and containing seats. The price of admission to the pit was one Elizabethan penny, while proportionately higher charges were made for the balconies. When it was wet the performance was postponed until the next day.

The stage was large, which made it easy to show crowd and battle scenes, and they are thus frequent in Elizabethan drama. It jutted far into the pit; hence it made no difference that people stood at the side of the stage as well as in front. It was without scenery and any but the most meagre properties. The scenery was created in the imagination of the audience by the words of the characters in the play: it was made part of the play so as not to obtrude and destroy the illusion of reality.

The play went straight on without intervals. Lack of intervals and frequent changes of scene were immaterial when the stage was without scenery, consequently a short scene or even a succession of short scenes is quite common in Elizabethan drama. It should be remembered that on Shakespeare's stage there were no separate scenes *as such*. In the early part of the present century his plays were presented with elaborate scenery, and sometimes the audience would

become impatient at the constant delays while it was being changed. At the present time there is a return to a simple stage setting, in keeping with that of Shakespeare's day, as, for instance, at the Royal Shakespeare Theatre, Stratford-on-Avon. There is good reason to believe that when they were first produced the plays took considerably less time than they do today. The Prologue to *Romeo and Juliet*, for instance, refers to 'the two hours' traffic of our stage'.

The end of a scene was frequently marked by rhyming lines, but *The Winter's Tale* is unique among Shakespeare's plays in being without a single example of this.

Just as the scenery had to be *put into* the words of the play, so had entrances and exits to be arranged as *part of* the play. In a modern play an actor can get into position before the rise of the curtain, but on the open stage it would seem artificial if he walked on and then started his first speech, or finished the scene and then walked off. Such endings as I, 2, 'Come sir, away'; II, 1, 'Come, follow us'; III, 6; 'Go: fresh horses!' clear the stage and at the same time fit in perfectly naturally with the action of the play. It follows that 'dead' bodies always had to be carried off the stage in the action.

It was not unknown for the stage floor to be equipped with a trapdoor for the sudden appearance and disappearance of ghosts and spirits, and some theatres had a flying apparatus by which such could descend on the stage with the aid of ropes on runners. Under the stage was the orchestra, a very important feature of the Elizabethan theatre.

At the back of the stage was a recess, and this was curtained and could be shut off when desired. The recess would, no doubt, contain the statue of Hermione. The stage direction at the beginning of the scene (V, 3) says that the statue is 'curtained', and later we are told that 'Paulina draws back a curtain, and discovers Hermione standing like a statue'; Hermione was evidently standing on a pedestal. Above the recess was a balcony, which served for an upper room, castle walls and such scenes. The balcony, too, could be curtained off.

People who wanted to be in the public eye were able to hire stools actually on the stage itself. An extra payment entitled them to have their pipes lit by a page, thus showing to all and sundry that they were in a position to be attended. Such a privilege would be valued by country gentlemen who wanted it to be known that they had come up to town. It was a source of continual annoyance to playwrights that actors 'gagged' in order to please these aristocratic playgoers.

By law, women were not allowed to act. Consequently women's parts had to be taken by boys with unbroken voices. Considering the limited emotional range of a boy's voice, imagine a boy's rendering of Desdemona, of Cleopatra or of Lady Macbeth! This ban accounts for the few women's parts in plays of the period, though some were always introduced for the sake of variety. In *The Winter's Tale*, one of Shakespeare's last plays, there are more than usual. It also accounts for the large number of plays where a woman disguises herself as a page boy. It made it much easier for the producer; further, the audience was intrigued by a situation in which a character was pretending to be what he really was! In *The Merchant of Venice* every one of the women disguises herself as a man.

Plays were not acted in period costume, though frequently *some* attempt was made to suggest a period, and the result must often have been a bizarre compromise. Thus all Shakespeare's plays can be said to have been first acted in 'modern dress'. Although there was no scenery, managers spared no expense on the most lavish of costumes.

On days when the theatre was open a flag was flown from the turret, and when the play was about to begin a trumpet was sounded. The turret of the Globe Theatre housed a big alarum bell, a favourite theatrical effect.

The text of Shakespeare's plays

Few readers of Shakespeare realize the difficulties that scholars have had to overcome in order to establish accurate texts of the plays. The First Folio, which contained thirty-six plays, is the basis of all subsequent editions. Other collected editions or Folios were published later in the seventeenth century, the Third and Fourth Folios containing seven additional plays, none of which, with the exception of *Pericles*, is now thought to be by Shakespeare. Sixteen of the plays had already been published separately as Quartos before 1623, and in the case of some plays, for example, *Hamlet*, more than one Quarto edition exists.

Some of the Quartos are almost word for word the same as the texts in the First Folio and were possibly set up from Shakespeare's own manuscript or at least from accurate theatre copies; but others are shortened, inferior versions, possibly 'pirated' editions published by some unauthorized person who had access to theatre copies of parts of them, or who had taken down the plays in shorthand while they were being performed. It is thought that the texts of the First Folio were set up from the good Quartos and from good theatre copies. But these texts must all be compared, printers' mistakes and other interference traced, before a reliable text can be arrived at.

The first editor to attempt the problem of the text was Nicholas Rowe (1674–1718), who also divided most of the plays into acts and scenes, supplied place-names of the location of each scene, indications of entrances and exits and a list of dramatis personae, which are absent from many of the texts in the Quarto and Folio editions. Rowe's divisions are convenient for reference (like the division of the books of the Bible into chapters and verses) but have no important use in

Shakespearean study. They were fitted for the stage of his time, but would have been to no purpose upon Shakespeare's stage with the barest of scenery.

While knowledge of the text is important for examination study, it should never be forgotten that the literary and dramatic aspects of the play are more vital. At the same time, study of the text is the basis of all literary and dramatic study.

The play

Plot

Leontes, King of Sicily, has been entertaining his lifelong friend, Polixenes, King of Bohemia, and falls victim to a senseless suspicion that his Queen, Hermione, whom everyone respects, has been having an affair with Polixenes. One of his closest counsellors is commissioned to murder Polixenes, but instead he informs Polixenes of the plot and hurries off with him back to his own country.

Their flight, however, increases Leontes' suspicions, and Hermione is publicly accused and sent off to gaol to await trial. Meanwhile, to justify himself, Leontes has sent messengers to consult the oracle of Apollo, but is so sure of his judgement that he proceeds, without its dispensation, to act as if Hermione were guilty. He disowns her daughter born in prison, and gives orders for the child to be abandoned in a 'remote and desert place'. It is abandoned in Bohemia and is found by a shepherd.

At the trial of Hermione, Leontes outrages all sensible opinion; but the proceedings are cut short by the arrival of the messengers with Apollo's 'oracle'. The oracle pronounces in favour of Hermione. At first Leontes breaks out 'There is no truth at all i' the oracle,' but at that very moment news is brought of the death of his son, which summarily fulfils one prophecy of the oracle. Leontes is at once convinced of his own injustice. Hermione swoons when she hears of the death of her son, and a little later Leontes is told that she too is dead. He gives himself up to years of mourning.

At this point there is a gap of sixteen years in the play. Hermione's abandoned daughter has grown into an attractive young woman, Perdita, in the home of the Bohemian shepherd; and is secretly courted by none other than Florizel, the son of King Polixenes. The King discovers his son's attachment to a shepherd's daughter and gives orders for it to cease.

Florizel prefers his love to his future throne, however, and, accompanied by Perdita, makes for the court of Leontes in Sicily, chased by his father. There, the Shepherd, who by accident has been shipped to Sicilia as well, proves that Perdita is the daughter of Leontes. Hermione, thought to be dead, turns out to be still alive, and the play ends with a happy reconciliation of all those who have been separated; and the promise of the union of the two royal families.

Source of plot and treatment

The plot of *The Winter's Tale* Shakespeare found in Robert Greene's novel *Pandosto, the Triumph of Time*, first published in 1588 but reprinted in 1607 and 1609. In view of the date of the play (see p.vii) it may have been the reprint which first drew Shakespeare's attention to it.

In essentials Shakespeare's story is the same, but there are many significant alterations of detail. All the characters are given new names and the kingdoms over which the two kings reign are reversed: in Greene, Pandosto (Leontes) is King of Bohemia and his visitor King of Sicilia. Shakespeare took over the sea-coast of Bohemia (which has brought him so many gibes) from Greene, though, in Greene, Perdita is cast adrift in an open boat at the mercy of the waves. Shakespeare gave Bohemia a desert (as well as a sea-coast) in which Perdita could be abandoned. In Greene, the Lords believe that Bellaria (Hermione) is guilty; whereas in *The Winter's Tale* their confidence in her innocence disposes the audience to the same view. In Greene, Bellaria defends her innocence; in Shakespeare Hermione takes it for granted and says comparatively little, and that little quietly, for honour not for life. This makes her more dignified. In Greene it is Bellaria who appeals to the oracle in the first place; whereas in Shakespeare Leontes seeks its justification (his conscience is uneasy), and Hermione does not mention the oracle until Cleomenes and

Dion have returned. In Greene there are two trials, which Shakespeare combines for dramatic concentration of interest. (Compare his subordination of the recognition of Perdita to that of Hermione – see p.8) Shakespeare makes Hermione live, whereas in Greene she really dies of shock on hearing of the death of her son – as she is reported to do in Shakespeare.

When the two runaway lovers seek sanctuary in a foreign land, Greene has Florizel cast into gaol; but Shakespeare wants everything to end happily, and enlists Leontes' sympathy on his side. Shakespeare's taste is better, for in Greene Pandosto makes passionate love to his unrecognized daughter and is with difficulty repelled. Then, when he finds out who she really is, he commits suicide. The ending of *The Winter's Tale* is to be a happy one, and all the main characters are to live and be restored to one another – Leontes without a further blemish (even if unwitting) on his character. The statue scene is entirely Shakespeare's own, of course, since, in Greene, Bellaria died at her trial.

Shakespeare's country scenes are not mere *literary* pastoralism, as Greene's are: they have the breath of the Stratford countryside about them. While it is difficult to point to specific differences, the difference in spirit can be felt at once. Shakespeare's country bumpkins, to say nothing of the rogue Autolycus, are the sort of country people he had met round Stratford. Greene had only *read* about the countryside.

Finally, the difference in title is suggestive. The name of the chief character is not the title of Shakespeare's play (as it often is; for example *Macbeth*, *Hamlet*, *Cymbeline*, etc.). He admits that the plot is beyond belief, and disarms criticism by calling it a 'Winter's Tale'. 'A sad tale's best for winter,' says Mamillius, and the Third Gentleman says that the story of the restoration of Perdita is 'like an old tale still, *which will have matter to rehearse, though credit be asleep*', and Paulina uses the same words of the restoration of Hermione – 'Like an old tale'.

It would be a mistake to think that his borrowing of the

story's outline detracts in any way from Shakespeare's genius:
the plot is the most unimportant part of a play. Shakespeare's
great artistic power is in characterization, so that a story which
in inferior hands would be crude and improbable becomes real
and lifelike. Invention is not the great artistic quality, but
insight – the conception the artist has of life as a whole. A story
with a 'realistic' plot has no life if the characters are wooden,
but a crude plot becomes alive when living people inform it.
Shakespeare was often very careless in his plots; it is in his *use*
of the plot that he shows his imagination. Artistic creation
bears the same relation to plot as does architecture to bricks
and mortar.

The plot of *The Winter's Tale* is no exception. It is generally
thin, to say the least, and full of inconsistencies. The motivating
force of the play is Leontes' suspicion of his wife and his best
friend; and this is so sudden and senseless as to be incredible.
A sudden whim shatters years of trust. The effect of the intervention of the oracle is discussed elsewhere (p.10): this removes
the cause of events from the effect of human character and
action, to an arbitrary outside force. Leontes says that 'one
grave shall be for both' his queen and his son, but the funeral
of Hermione was either forgotten or it was a sham. The loss
of the mariners and Antigonus from different causes in the self-
same moment is indeed a coincidence, and it is strange that
the bear bothered to chase a tough old man when a tender
babe lay ready on the grass.

The stratagem of bringing in Time as a Chorus is less
dramatic than making the audience realize the passage of
time from the words and appearances of some of the characters whom they have already met. Shakespeare usually did
this in the speech of minor characters. Here he takes the easy
way out (see p.6).

The meeting of Prince and Princess is no greater coincidence
than is met with in many a stock fairy story, and is made
credible by the nature of Perdita, who has a queenly presence.

That is, the plot is made credible by *the human characters that inform it*, whereas the impulse of Leontes at the beginning of the play is out of character and for that reason is difficult to believe in. It is curious that Florizel fails to recognize his father in disguise, especially as he was accompanied by Camillo. Camillo offers to fix up a royal reception in Sicilia for Florizel and Perdita, although he has not been there for sixteen years. Florizel has a ship ready when he makes up his mind to run away with Perdita to Sicily.

> And most opportune to our need I have
> A vessel rides fast by, but not prepar'd
> For this design.

The Shepherd must have been very obtuse not to have told Polixenes his story as soon as Polixenes revealed who he was, or to have been carried off to Sicilia against his will.

On Hermione's side, it is most improbable that she would be willing to be shut up for sixteen years in the prime of life, when she knew that Leontes was ready at any time to receive her back with honour and respect. She certainly did not do it to punish him. Neither could she have known that in due course her lost daughter would be restored to her. It is strange that Paulina could visit 'that removed house' where Hermione was concealed, 'twice or thrice a day' for sixteen years, without people talking. It is even more strange that, at the end, Leontes – who has for sixteen years yearned daily for Hermione – raises no voice in condemnation of Paulina who had kept her away from him. Or perhaps in his new happiness he thinks that it has been Hermione's wish, and it is best to accept what has come and not rake up the past. Inconsistencies in character depiction are discussed in the appropriate places, however.

It is perhaps possible to imagine that a living person is a statue, if one is in the right surroundings and is not allowed to touch. People have made this, and the opposite, mistake at Madame Tussaud's waxworks exhibition. But the statue scene must be done very carefully and sympathetically, or it can easily degenerate into a joke. The marriage of Camillo and Paulina, arbitrarily added, (see p.7) is superfluous: the only marriage we are interested in is that of Florizel and Perdita. Shakespeare here fails to keep the sense of proportion he showed when he subordinated the recognition of the lost Perdita to that of her mother (see p.8).

Much has been made by critics of Bohemia's 'sea-shore', alongside 'a desert', but such inaccuracies are not peculiar to this play: carelessness over unimportant detail is thoroughly Shakespearean.

The Winter's Tale is, as its title suggests, a tale for the fireside rather than a picture of life. Thus, while the student must be aware of its improbabilities, it would be rather pedantic to take objection to the story.

Construction

The construction of *The Winter's Tale* is perhaps the most random of that in any of Shakespeare's plays.

The most striking feature of the play is the gap of sixteen years between Acts III and IV: not only this; other new characters are introduced in Act IV, and Leontes is dropped for a time – he does not appear between Act III Scene 2 and Act V Scene 1. The play covers a long period of years; lacks unity and a sense of cohesion; and the main events occur suddenly, giving us a surprise we are not prepared for. Although the events of the play stretch over so long a period, in no other Shakespeare play do they move more quickly.

The gap is managed, not dramatically by reference in the speeches of minor characters, but *from outside* by a Chorus, introduced specifically to narrate events not shown on the stage. This device is unusual in Shakespeare. He is getting careless, and he takes the line of least resistance. It is interesting to note that the action of *The Tempest*, the play Shakespeare wrote next to *The Winter's Tale* (immediately afterwards, perhaps immediately before) is compressed into three hours; which shows his versatility – he can turn his hand to a play of either very long or very short duration. Incidentally, in contrast with that of *The Winter's Tale*, the plot of *The Tempest* is a well-knit one.

The tearing of Antigonus by the bear is the most ludicrous incident in Shakespeare. It is harrowing, not tragic, because it is accidental and unrelated to either the character or actions of Antigonus. Hence we do not sympathize with him; and his fatal misadventure comes near to making us laugh. (e.g. '*Exit, pursued by a bear.*' Act III Scene 3 line 57, is sprung upon the reader quite without warning or preparation.) Shakespeare must have been aware of this effect, but was in no mood to care. Also, the marriage of Camillo and Paulina is a most unnatural incident: a marriage between two people who had never spoken to one another, forced on them from without, in the absence of any apparent inclination on their part – again an 'accidental' happening, unrelated to the character or actions of the two participants. The first event was to get rid of Antigonus; the other to give a 'happy ending' all round!

Allowing for these major weaknesses the construction of the play has characteristic Shakespearean features. It has a typical opening scene in which the main characters are discussed by two lesser people, who tell one another what they both know, for the benefit of the audience. In Shakespeare's early plays the main characters appeared on the stage at the outset, e.g. in the History plays. Later on, however, e.g. *Twelfth Night* (1601) onwards, he generally leads up to them in the conversation of minor characters, which is dramatically much more effective. The situation is built up before the main characters enter; and this method also has the advantage of creating suspense, so that when they appear they do so in response to a longing of the audience to see them. From a practical point of view it also means that the first speeches of the main characters are not disturbed by the entrance of late-arriving theatregoers: by the time they speak, the audience has 'settled down'.

The individual scenes in the two halves of the play (it is significant that one can thus divide the play) are well linked. For instance, Act I ends with the flight of Polixenes and Camillo; and in the first scene of Act II the fury of Leontes is increased by the news of their flight. Most of the other scenes are similarly closely connected, and reference is made to this in the Notes (e.g. pp.53 and 54).

Contrast in tone sets off a tragic scene. For instance, just before Leontes bursts in on Hermione with his accusation, she is chattering pleasantly with her boy, much as in *Macbeth* Lady Macduff is playing with her son before the murderers sent by Macbeth descend on both to make away with them. Similarly before the trial scene there is a quiet scene, where Cleomenes and Dion talk together of their impressions – 'The climate's delicate, the air most sweet'. This again is very similar to the scene in *Macbeth*, where Duncan comments on the attractive situation of Macbeth's house,

> This castle hath a pleasant seat; the air
> Nimbly and sweetly recommends itself
> Unto our gentle senses.

The scene from *The Winter's Tale* is, however, without the piercing dramatic irony of the above. The scenes add nothing to the plot of their play, they are there for atmosphere only. In Act IV Scene 3 comedy and tragedy, or at least comic and serious, jostle one another all the way through (as they do, indeed, in life) and help to relieve one another and at the same time to throw one another up.

With admirable dramatic insight the recognition of Perdita is told at second hand, not presented. Had it not been so it would have taken attention away from the main recognition scene, that of Hermione, which would have come as an anti-climax. Everything is subordinated to the recognition of

Hermione; the recognition of Perdita is *told*, and *by a minor character, in prose and in affected court diction.* Furthermore, the audience is aware of Perdita's identity; but there has been no clue in the play that Hermione is still alive. In the statue's return to life Shakespeare planned as big a surprise for the audience as for the characters on stage.

The songs in the play, like most of those in Shakespeare, are not introduced merely to show off the vocal accomplishments of a member of the theatrical company, but have a direct relation to the plot (and atmosphere) of the play.

Atmosphere and theme

The theme of the play would seem to be forgiveness (after repentance) and reconciliation – after three Acts of relentless bitterness and senseless hatred. This is the theme of *Cymbeline* and *The Tempest*, which also belong to the last period of Shakespeare's career. His temper during this period wanted a peaceful ending. His outlook on life was softened. John Masefield calls it 'the gentlest of Shakespeare's plays.'

The play ends in 'great comfort', and a tragic ending, violently threatened in the first part, is purposely avoided – in fact, Shakespeare alters his source to do so. The period of bitter tragedy is over for Shakespeare and the serenity of one who has risen from its dark depths casts sweetness and light over human relations. There is a strange other-worldliness about these last comedies, so different from the gay brilliance of the earlier ones (e.g. *As You Like It*), that they have been called 'Romances'. The plays show a delight in youth; but Perdita and Imogen and Miranda are more ethereal creatures than Rosalind and Celia. The effect is of old and far-off things, at a time 'when age and forgetfulness sweeten memory'.* It is as if Shakespeare looks on these things and does not hope to possess them.

Murder in the Cathedral, T. S. Eliot

In the earlier comedies matters come right by virtue of a certain tendency of human nature towards physical and moral health; whereas in *The Winter's Tale* and *Cymbeline* (both plays dealing with the wrongs done by man to woman) they are righted not so much from within as by divine intervention (the oracle of Apollo) from without. Without the oracle's message, Leontes would never have felt the remorse of a guilty soul.

The sufferers in the later plays are more mature: riper and deeper in mind, with more capacity for feeling. As a result, the tragic element strikes deeper and affects the spectator more profoundly. All the 'romantic comedies' are weightier. In the earlier comedies suffering comes to people with young vivacious spirits that help them to take it less to heart. Shakespeare's mood now may still be bright but it is no longer sparkling: there is a tender, mellow, autumnal tone over all these last plays. In the second half of the play – though not in the first – tragic foreboding is skilfully lightened by comic relief and the charming fresh country scenes where Perdita is 'the queen of curds and cream', handing 'the fairest flowers o' the season' to her guests. As the play nears its end in the impressive statue scene, beautiful music blends with and intensifies the atmosphere of enchantment.

The play has an aristocratic outlook. Everyone wonders how an attractive, well-bred girl can possibly be a shepherd's daughter; and it turns out that their wonder has good foundation. By implication, Florizel is attracted to Perdita because he intuitively senses that she is a gentlewoman born. By implication, Perdita does not give up Florizel at the King's command, but consents to run off with him because she inwardly feels his equal (notwithstanding that her decision endangers the life of her 'father'). Florizel's renunciation of his throne for his love would have impressed the audience more had she really been a shepherd's daughter. But this prejudice against the common man (or woman) is general in the literature of an age when rank had more power and privilege than in our day, and is typical of Shakespeare's plays as a whole.

Setting

The local colour of all Shakespeare's plays is that of Elizabethan England, whether the story be one of Sicily and Bohemia, Britain or Denmark, and in whatever age. Nowadays we would demand strict accuracy in scenery, costume and topical references; but then, for playwright and audience alike, the life and spirit of a play mattered more than strict accuracy in local colour. 'It is the spirit which giveth life.' People saw in the drama a reflection of their own life and experience; its appeal was in no wise analytical or educational, but human.

Further, in those days people were untravelled and uneducated and would not recognize anachronisms on which a certain type of modern critic loves to pounce.

And it must be remembered that there was neither scenery nor period costume. Incongruities that become apparent beside 'realistic' scenery would not have been noticed then. In references to a character's dress it would be farcical if the references were historically correct –, but to something the character was not actually wearing on the stage!

The Winter's Tale takes place nominally in Sicily and Bohemia at an unspecified time, but we are really never far from the England Shakespeare knew. The local colour is all Elizabethan, the sheep-shearing revels especially so. The food (Act IV Scene 2), the flowers, the pedlar's wares (Act IV Scene 3), the costumes (not to mention the pencilled eyebrows – Act II Scene 1 line 13) are straight from the England of Elizabeth I (or James I). We hear of 'wakes, fairs and bear-baitings'; an 'ape-bearer'; a puppet show of the Prodigal Son (Act IV Scene 2); tabor, pipe and ballads; gossip at the kiln-hole (Act IV Scene 3); while the rich man enjoys himself in hunting and falconry (Act III Scene 3 and Act IV Scene 3). The popularity of the masque in the early seventeenth century is mentioned on page 71, and, apart from the 'dance of twelve Satyrs', Autolycus sells 'masks for faces'. Tinkers, bailiffs and 'process-servers' are well-known people (Act IV Scene 2) and constables and beadles are thoroughly Elizabethan. To rogues like Autolycus the stocks and the gallows are a very real danger.

Puritans and Whitsun pastorals are to be found in Bohemia at the same time as Apollo's Oracle at Delphi is consulted in Sicily, both in the life of Julio Romano (see note, p.69), and while an emperor reigns in Russia. The rich and educated, as well as the superstitious poor, believe that the stars have an influence upon their lives (Act II Scene 1 line 101).

But more important than specific allusions like these is the Elizabethan atmosphere throughout. All the country scenes have a strongly Elizabethan flavour, and the sheep-shearing scenes give us the essence of country life in and around the Stratford-on-Avon in which Shakespeare grew up. Altogether, the play gives as true a cross-section of Elizabethan life as any play on an avowedly contemporary topic.

Characters

Leontes

'I am a feather for each wind that blows'

The characters of *The Winter's Tale*, Leontes in particular, are less convincing than those of the great Shakespearean tragedies. For years Leontes has never had reason to question the devotion of Hermione or the friendship of Polixenes, yet all in a moment his trust in both is overthrown. And the cause is nothing but his own petty jealousy, magnified out of all proportion. The first trace of his jealousy is seen when Polixenes agrees to stay on as his guest at Hermione's request, although he had declined at Leontes': 'At my request he would not'. The motive of every deed and word of Hermione and

Polixenes after that is distorted in the light of his suspicion, and when Hermione innocently says

> Why, lo you now, I have spoke to the purpose twice:
> The one for ever earn'd a royal husband;
> The other for some while a friend.

Leontes misinterprets her words as an indication of the worst – 'Too hot, too hot!' It is incredible that a sensible man would suffer a long and worthwhile affection to be jeopardized without some further investigation. The trouble is that his pride has been hurt, and he determines to make both Hermione and Polixenes suffer for it, notwithstanding that he himself has urged Hermione to supplement his pleading with Polixenes (of which he is indeed reminded). He gave Hermione an implied reproach that she failed to persuade Polixenes to stay (Act I Scene 2 line 27), whereupon she replied

> I had thought, sir, to have held my peace until
> You had drawn oaths from him not to stay.

and he praised her for her good sense. When Hermione and Polixenes have gone (at his request) his wounded pride can have full fling, when there is only a subordinate to listen to him! In those days kings could indulge their silly fancies with impunity, and it was not always safe, let alone wise, to disagree with them. As Camillo says, Leontes is 'One who in rebellion with himself, will have all that are his so too'. Nevertheless, Camillo, to his credit, does stand up for Hermione, but his views are treated with contempt and he is stilled with a curt contradiction.

> You lie, you lie:
> I say thou liest, Camillo, and I hate thee;

(See note on 'thou', p.41). Notice how repetition helps to assure him that his delusion is true. If Camillo pursues his difference with the king he is a dead man, too, so he agrees before Leontes' face to poison Polixenes, but gets out of it by running away with him. Unfortunately Camillo unwittingly puts things in such a way as to fan the king's suspicion:

> He would not stay at your petitions; made
> His business more material.

and he goes on to say that Polixenes changed his mind 'At the good queen's entreaty'. Camillo's running away, of course, lends colour to Leontes' suspicions. But the king betrays a guilty conscience by his euphemisms.

>   If I
> Had servants true about me, ... they would do that
> Which should undo more doing: ay, and thou,
> His cupbearer ... might'st bespice a cup,
> To give mine enemy a lasting wink;

Further, he is hesitant when he first mentions his wife's 'slipperiness' to Camillo.

Everyone admires Hermione, but the king is deaf to all entreaty. When at first he orders her to be taken to prison, no one stirs – people cannot believe their ears. One would imagine that he would stop and think when his own view conflicted with the view of all his court. Instead of that, opposition establishes his delusion all the more firmly – he will show them that he is right and that he cannot be opposed. When a Lord dissents (on the stage he is shown to be the spokesman of all the lords) he is told

>   Our prerogative
> Calls not your counsels; but our natural goodness
> Imparts this: which, if you, – or stupified
> Or seeming so in skill, – cannot or will not
> Relish a truth, like us, inform yourselves
> We need no more of your advice;

But for his position, Leontes would be despised. His supicion grows by what it feeds on. He makes wild charges – 'There

is a plot against my life, my crown.' He accuses Hermione in
front of the whole court, and in front of her own son, a cruel
thing to do. An innocent babe is condemned to death to
satisfy his vengeance against its mother and supposed father.
He announces his intention of going further and speaking
against Hermione 'in public'. He has no sympathy for her
feelings. When Hermione swoons, upon the news of her son's
death, Leontes casually says

> Take her hence:
> Her heart is but o'ercharg'd; she will recover:
> I have too much believ'd mine own suspicion:
> Beseech you, tenderly apply to her
> Some remedies for life.

– It's nothing, she will soon be better, and he goes on to say
that he will soon put matters right – everything will soon be
forgotten. When he makes another wild charge, that Antigonus has 'set on' his wife to protest against the murder of
Hermione's babe, and it is shown that the charge can be dis-
proved, Leontes does not attempt to reason, any more than
he did with Camillo in Act I, he simply falls back on his
superior position and tries to silence the lords with 'You're
liars all'. Leontes is a creature of fits and starts. In a moment
he varies the fate of Hermione and that of her child. He loses
his grip on himself. Paulina with reason refers to 'These
dangerous unsafe lunes i' the king' (though she is thinking only
of the punishment of Hermione). Even when he consults the
oracle, he does so with his mind made up, and calls that a
liar too— 'There is no truth at all i' the oracle.' He sends
Hermione's child to be abandoned *before* he knows the verdict
of the oracle. One might reasonably ask why he bothered to
send to it. It is quite obvious that had the oracle agreed with
him he would have published its findings as divine approval.
He was glad to hide behind an appearance of fairness—

> Let us be clear'd
> Of being tyrannous, since we so openly
> Proceed in justice.

But when one part of the prophecy of the oracle is so dramatically fulfilled by the death of Mamillius, Leontes gives in all at once, in as surprising a fashion as he has stood his ground so far.

For a time we leave him, yet before the play closes we feel sorry for the lonely old man*, in mind of his sin every day of his life. He has learnt something and is mellowed by the years. Contrition always arouses sympathy, however great the sin, and we respect him as he says before the 'statue',

> I am ashamed: does not the stone rebuke me
> For being more stone than it?

Now he submits to the taunts of Paulina without remonstrance, or at least with only a request to her to 'say so but seldom', and agrees that he killed Hermione when Paulina puts it that way. He does not threaten her with fire now, but considers that her reproaches have been a 'great comfort'; he no doubt feels that it has done him good to have his wounds kept green. He is shown at his best in humble repentance and genuine gratitude, as he regains the wife he need never have lost.

Polixenes
'Your guest'

Polixenes does not make so strong an impression as Leontes. He is important only in so far as he affects other people. He is really Leontes in reverse. In the sixteen years' space of time covered by the play he gets worse as Leontes gets better. He behaves like a gentleman in Act I, but sixteen years later he

---

*Leontes appears older than he really is. He was grey bearded before he was forty, in the first part of the play (Act II Scene 3 line 161).

sets spies on his son, acts as a spy himself, and threatens to have the old shepherd hanged and Perdita's 'beauty scratch'd with briers'.

> If ever henceforth thou
> These rural latches to his entrance open,
> Or hoop his body more with thy embraces,
> I will devise a death as cruel for thee
> As thou art tender to 't.

Just like Leontes he softens after this angry outburst, and remands the shepherd and Perdita to see how things go. He shows much more self-control as a younger man charged with adultery than he does as an elderly father to the country girl who has captured his son's heart. He unthinkingly submits his son and heir to unnecessary indignities, and after his son's escape implores Leontes to arrest him. Camillo, who judged Leontes' character so well, speaks of Polixenes' 'fury'.

It has been pointed out by some editors that Polixenes is inconsistent in argument, drawing Perdita's attention to the way grafting 'A gentler scion to the wildest stock' improves the strain, and failing to see that the same thing will happen if Florizel marries Perdita. It is rather far-fetched, however, for anyone to wish to apply horticultural methods to human reproduction. This speech of Polixenes' is obviously inserted for its dramatic irony in that connection, however. But, as Shakespeare himself does not believe it, everyone in the theatre knows that Perdita is really 'a gentler scion' too.

Perhaps it is not surprising, then, that Polixenes and Leontes were such great friends in early life, for they had much in common. But between two such intolerant natures a break is sure to come sooner or later. Despotic kings (tyrants, some would call them) are accustomed to have their own way, and hence cannot bear to be crossed. Polixenes himself says (of Leontes), 'As his passion's mighty, must it [his jealousy] be violent'. The same applies equally well to himself.

Polixenes is not one of the most important characters in the play, but he is considered here next to Leontes to facilitate comparison between the two.

Hermione
'A precious creature'

Without Hermione *The Winter's Tale* would have but little charm. Yet the deep impression made by her is out of all proportion to her few appearances in the play. It comes as rather a surprise to realize that she appears in only four scenes and speaks fewer than two hundred lines. In spite of this, her influence is felt throughout the play.

We meet her as a loving wife and mother, happy to extend the hospitality of her household to her husband's friend. She is playful and full of fun (e.g. Act I Scene 2 lines 89–101), though she soon finds a child's play 'past enduring' (Act II Scene 1 lines 1–2), but in this connection, to be fair, it should be remembered that she was not in normal health. Then suddenly, through the insensate jealousy of her husband, she is accused of being an unfaithful wife and, deprived of her children, cannot act as a mother. From the three people who meant all the world to her she is barred.

In adversity she is patient and self-possessed, and shows none of her husband's panicky whims.

> I must be patient till the heavens look
> With an aspect more favourable. Good my lords,
> I am not prone to weeping ... but I have
> That honourable grief lodg'd here which burns
> Worse than tears drown.

Though she knows herself grossly wronged, she submits to the king's will – 'And so the king's will be performed!'

At her trial Hermione is quiet and dignified and she reasons well. Her quietness emphasizes her sincerity. Sincere natures are not noisy and declamatory. Her speech is calm and composed by the side of Leontes' fits and starts. Loss of honour means more to her than loss of life (Act III Scene 2 lines 43–46, 110–111). Life without 'The crown and comfort of my life' – Leontes' favour – is lost already. Yet in 'The flatness of her misery' she calls for pity, not revenge. The way in which she bears her suffering is an inspiration.

Then she is hidden away. We have no inkling of what prompted her to consent to this long seclusion, which must have been a living death, and was pointless once Leontes was repentant. This incident, however, does not arise from her character; it is one of the absurdities of the plot and we are left in the dark about Hermione's views upon it. Suffice it to say that when it is over she embraces her husband affectionately though, be it noted, she does not speak to him when he addresses her. She speaks only to the daughter she has not seen since birth. Her mother's heart wells up. But (though she does not mention it) she will not be able to enjoy the nearness of her daughter for long, for Perdita will soon be leaving her for a home of her own in a foreign land.

Perdita

> 'Nothing she does or seems
> But smacks of something greater than herself'

Perdita is an innocent girlish figure (see pp.10–11), who has been brought up in idealized surroundings. She takes no prominent part in the action of the play – she follows where others lead. She is remembered most for the speeches which show her love of flowers. Country-bred, she is natural and unsophisticated. She spurns the fashionable aids to beauty (e.g. make-up) she would have employed had she never been taken from court.

> No more than, were I painted, I would wish
> This youth should say 'twere well

She hates vulgarity and sends a warning to Autolycus to 'use
no scurrilous words in's tunes'. She lends grace to her cottage
and has a latent nobility which can be felt in spite of her
unfitting surroundings – she is 'Too noble for this place'. She
herself is unaware of her origin, but it is evident in spite of
herself.

She is deeply in love with Florizel, and forgets that she is
the hostess and retires to talk with him (Act IV Scene 3
lines 62–68). Once she wonders if she has been too forward
and said too much, so looks for an excuse.

> Methinks I play as I have seen them do
> In Whitsun pastorals: sure, this robe of mine
> Does change my disposition.

She is practical and straightforward.

> Your resolution cannot hold, when 'tis
> Oppos'd, as it must be, by the power of the king.

She had warned Florizel that her 'dignity would last, but till
'twere known'. She does not seek to trap him into marriage.
When the two young lovers are found out, and she has proof
that Florizel is in earnest, she loves him enough to fly with
him to a foreign country, when the choice has to be made.
Although (so far as she knows) she is a simple shepherdess, she
feels fit to take her place as Florizel's wife (see p.10), Shakespeare's way of saying that birth will out.

Added to all this, her physical attractiveness is unequalled,
and all who see her are struck by it. Polixenes, who is preju-
diced against her, cannot but admit that

> This is the prettiest low-born lass that ever
> Ran on the green-sward.

Her good fortune does not make her forget the father who has
brought her up, and in Sicilia she shows concern for him when
he is in trouble, questioned by Camillo and threatened by
Polixenes – 'O my poor father'.

In common with all Shakespeare's heroines, Perdita is (to all intents and purposes) motherless. The shepherd's wife has been dead a long time, presumably since before he found Perdita. (At all events, when he finds her he does not say to the clown, 'We will take her home to mother', as he would have done had she been alive.) The dramatic effect of this is to throw her on to her own resources – she has no other woman on whom she can rely; and this awakens our sympathy for her lonely hand. She does not quite come up to her 'father's' idea of a hostess (Act IV Scene 3 lines 55–70) and (more important) she has to make her own decision about Florizel.

Perdita and Florizel are a guarantee to Shakespeare that the world is sound. He builds his hopes on them. The eyes of the sufferers may rest on them with comfort: but they themselves do not come near the real suffering; they are remote from it and hardly conscious of it until it is all over.

At the end Shakespeare looks beyond the injuries of the present to the future happy union of the two families in the marriage of the two young lovers, who carry our minds forward to the next generation. In the half-light of the statue scene, with gentle music, the past seems like a nightmare; but as we look on Perdita and Florizel the future seems brighter. This note of hope at the end is characteristic of all Shakespeare's plays, not excluding the tragedies.

Paulina
'If I prove honey-mouth'd, let my tongue blister'

Paulina lives not because she is a consistent well-developed character, but because she is the centre of one or two great situations. She does not appear until Hermione has been put in prison, and is introduced to guide the feelings of the audience. She it is who is the only one courageous enough to front Leontes (Act III Scene 2). It is she who arranges the powerful statue scene (Act V Scene 3). She is a strong, forthright, managing woman of unassailable motives, but with insufficient tact to make her protests effective. She reproaches Leontes with withering scorn, but only makes him more angry and obstinate (Act II Scene 3). Since she has, apparently, been at court for a very long time, one would imagine her to have discovered a way to handle him better. She certainly showed little good sense, though plenty of courage, when she denounced him as a 'tyrant' (Act III Scene 2 line 208). She can scratch too – 'Let him that makes but trifles of his eyes first hand me'.

Considering that it was false she announces the death of the Queen in telling fashion. Indeed, she was false to the oath she swore it on. It should be remembered, however, that she has to convince the audience as well as the characters of the play that Hermione is dead (see p.3). Impulsive people like Paulina find it harder to keep secrets and not come out with what is in their heads. All the more credit to her that she so cleverly kept the secret of Hermione's seclusion within a stone's throw of Leontes. But what happened in those sixteen years should not be pressed as evidence of character. Shakespeare accepted the gap in the play, independent of the characters concerned. After the gap is over, Paulina cleverly gets Leontes to promise that he will wed only a queen of her choice.

It is unfortunate that Paulina gets fobbed off with Camillo, for whom she has shown no liking; and we have it only on flimsy hearsay that he is interested in her. This marriage is sprung on us. It does not develop out of the play: someone else fixes it up suddenly.

Autolycus
'A snapper-up of unconsidered trifles'

Autolycus has no place in Greene's *Pandosto*. He comes into Shakespeare's play straight from the English countryside. This is not the only play of Shakespeare's where we like the worst character the best. A light-fingered pickpocket, an expert trickster, he yet endears himself to us by his 'merry heart' and his nimble wit. He takes life as it comes, without worrying – ''tis all one to me' – and looks on the bright side of things. His breezy presence keeps us in good spirits. Incidentally, he sings some beautiful songs (see p.9), showing a real zest for life.

He steals only trifles, for 'Gallows and knock are too powerful on the highway'. He is no robber where the stakes are too great. Conscience has no part in this, however; the sin is in being found out and suffering punishment – 'beating and hanging are terrors to me'.

Quite apart from what he gets out of it, he enjoys fooling the simple country yokels he finds at the sheep-shearing feast. Mopsa 'loves a ballad in print ... for then we are sure they are true', whereupon Autolycus tells some of the 'tall stories' printed in his ballads, and must get a lot of fun out of the impression they make.

Really, Autolycus is independent of the main action of the plot. He is linked to it by having once been in the service of Prince Florizel, but this is casual and unnecessary. He fulfils the same dramatic function as the Fool in such plays as *Twelfth Night* and *As You Like It*, bringing comic relief of a witty and intelligent kind. In *The Winter's Tale* there is a Clown as well, but the student should beware of confusing the functions of the fool and the clown. The Clown in Shakespeare is not a jester, but a country yokel, quite unconscious of the fun he is causing. We laugh *at* the Clown, but *with* the Fool. The Clown in *The Winter's Tale* is a caricature. Autolycus is a character. The Clown is a rustic type, English and localized; the Fool can take his place at court. The Clown, however, is not always poor, as, for instance, Justice Shallow and Dogberry. The Clown is a victim of the situation; the Fool master. The Clown has less wit, the Fool more, than the 'gentlemen'. The professional Fool was, in fact, paid to amuse the 'gentlemen' by his wit. When the Fool comments on the situation he usually has a shrewder idea of things than most people, whereas the comments of the Clown are idiotic.

Some of Shakespeare's comic characters will not easily fit into one of these two pigeon-holes: for example young Gobbo (old Gobbo is obviously a Clown), but broadly speaking these are the differences.

Deception in *The Winter's Tale*

All the important characters of *The Winter's Tale* are deceitful at some point, with good or bad intent, and for convenience instances are listed together here.

Paulina carries out the major deception on which the plot depends. She deceives Leontes and all the rest of the court when she swears (on oath) that Hermione is dead, and again when she presents a 'statue' to bring her back to the world. Hermione is a party to this deceit.

Leontes deceives Polixenes, plotting his death while he is a guest in his palace. He deceives himself, of course, in face of all the evidence, about Hermione's guilt, but his self-deception is outside the scope of these examples and is discussed under his character (pp. 12–16).

Polixenes, in disguise, deceives Florizel and all present at the sheep-shearing feast.

Camillo deceives Leontes in escaping with Polixenes; Polixenes by encouraging and assisting the escape of Florizel and Perdita for his own ends; and Florizel and Perdita by immediately telling Polixenes of their escape.

Florizel and Perdita deceive their fathers by running off secretly. On his arrival in Sicilia Florizel (with the tacit approval of Perdita) deceives Leontes, spinning a plausible tale to account for his unannounced visit (Act V Scene 1 lines 159–168).

The Old Shepherd deceives Perdita by concealing from her that she was a foundling.

Autolycus deceives all and sundry. His whole life is a deception.

Style

Professor Dowden has an excellent summary of the development of Shakespeare's style.

In the earliest plays the language is sometimes as it were a dress put upon the thought – a dress ornamented with superfluous care; the idea is at times hardly sufficient to fill out the language in which it is put; in the middle of plays (*Julius Caesar* serves as an example) there seems a perfect balance and equality between the thought and its expression. In the latest plays this balance is disturbed by the preponderance or excess of the ideas over the means of giving them utterance. The sentences are close-packed; their 'rapid and abrupt turnings of thought, so quick that language can hardly follow fast enough; impatient activity of intellect and fancy, which, having once disclosed an idea, cannot wait to work it orderly out'; 'the language is sometimes alive with imagery'.*

All these characteristics of the latest plays are present in *The Winter's Tale*. Shakespeare often expresses more in a sentence than seems possible. It has many elliptical passages, whose meaning is difficult to extricate, e.g.

> More than mistress of
> Which comes to me in name of fault I must not
> At all acknowledge,

or

> But that the good mind of Camillo tardied
> My swift command, though I with death and with
> Reward did threaten and encourage him,
> Not doing it and being done.

* *Shakespeare Primer*, page 37 (see our footnote, p.vii)

Dramatically such a style is inferior, as it is difficult to understand the thought at the speed at which it is spoken.

But the *form* of Shakespeare's mature verse is far superior dramatically, making the dialogue more natural and more adapted to different characters. Many lines are 'run-on', that is, the sense of one line is completed in the next and there is no stop at the end of the line; the stronger pauses are placed within the line at different points; many lines have extra unaccented syllables. Florizel's speech to Camillo, beginning 'So call it', in the middle of Act IV Scene 3, is a good example of Shakespeare's later style.

Graphic and figurative language abounds in the play and the richness and vividness of the imagery is to be noted. The similes and metaphors have that sense of surprise and yet of fitness which characterizes the imagery of a genius. Sometimes simile and metaphor succeed one another quickly or are interwoven in one conception (e.g. Act IV Scene 3 lines 1–5, or the oft-quoted lines, 118–124). Some of the most beautiful imagery comes appropriately in the talk of the two young lovers, Florizel and Perdita, imagery close to nature. Figurative language is not only more beautiful but more powerful than a mere prosaic statement. Look at the force of Leontes' metaphors as he remembers his wife's eyes.

> Stars, stars,
> And all eyes else dead coals!

Many passages from the play are worth committing to memory, and for convenience these are listed separately on p.94.

In a good play the style naturally reflects the character of the person speaking, and even the same man in two different moods may speak in two different ways. Look at Leontes' broken, hesitant speech when he first suggests to Camillo that Hermione is 'slippery' (Act I Scene 2 lines 267–279); or his abrupt and disjointed speech when he accuses Hermione in public (Act III Scene 2 lines 81–88). Similarly, Leontes' unsteady mind is also emphasized by quick changes of metaphor, e.g. Act II Scene 3 lines 2–9. In contrast, Hermione's speeches are measured and regular.

The speech of Time in the Chorus at the beginning of Act IV is differentiated from the main play by being in the form of rhyming couplets. The normal line in Shakespeare's plays is a blank-verse iambic pentameter. Apart from this technical difference the whole tone of Time's speech is very pedestrian. The songs of Autolycus are of course, appropriately, in shorter rhyming lines, except for one in stanza form.

There are fashions in literature as in everything else. In Elizabethan times punning was extremely popular, and this kind of verbal trickery is prevalent in Shakespeare's earlier work; but, apart from the speeches of Autolycus – who thoroughly enjoyed a pun – there are fewer puns in *The Winter's Tale* than is usual in Shakespeare.

Use of Prose

The normal form of Shakespeare's plays is blank verse. When prose is used, it is for a definite purpose.

Prose is invariably used for

1 Comic characters (e.g. Autolycus and the Clown) and

2 Characters of lower social position (e.g. the Servant)
This was a literary convention at a time when literature was aristocratic and the chief characters in plays (as in life) were kings and nobles. Scenes in which the lower orders of society figure are used as a contrast; these people live on a lower plane of feeling than the main characters, and thereby emphasize the height of the feeling of the main characters; and the contrast in the medium of expression – prose instead of verse is in perfect keeping.

Sometimes the reason for prose is a lower pitch of feeling

without a lower social position in the speaker. The first scene of the play is in prose, for instance, because it is a lead up to the main play – the two speakers are surveying affairs as from a distance, without the sharp feeling which develops later. Act IV Scene 1 bears the same relation to the second half of the play.

It is not in accordance with Shakespeare's usual custom that the Gaoler and the Mariner speak in verse (Act II Scene 2 and Act III Scene 3). Possibly Shakespeare has given the Gaoler verse to show an unexpressed sympathy with his noble prisoner, but the Mariner makes no reference to Perdita (unless his last speech is a reference to her fate), so that the purpose of his speaking in verse cannot be to imply sympathetic feeling with her.

The Old Shepherd talks in prose when he is alone with his son (Act III Scene 3) or speaking to a servant (Act IV Scene 3), but in verse when in the presence of visitors of distinction. It is instructive to notice that the only three lines of verse spoken by Autolycus are when he is *pretending to be* a 'courtier cap-a-pe'. Camillo talks in verse with Perdita and Florizel, but almost in the same breath in prose to Autolycus (Act IV Scene 3). Finally, Perdita, although believed to be of 'low' birth, emphasizes her latent inborn nobility by speaking in verse at all times, except for one sentence to a servant, and the 'noble' characters recognize it implicitly by addressing her in verse.

3 Formal proclamations, letters etc. (e.g. the indictment of Hermione and the oracle of Apollo).

Notes and revision questions

Act I Scene 1

Polixenes, King of Bohemia, is on a state visit to Leontes, King of Sicily. In Leontes' palace a Sicilian Lord talks with a Lord of Bohemia about the enduring friendship between their respective kings.

This short introductory scene is very important, as the whole course of events develops from the friendship between the two monarchs. See also p.7.

Bohemia Corresponding roughly to the present-day Czechoslovakia, though Shakespeare had no particular place in mind (see p.6).

the like occasion A similar errand

Sicilia Sicily, an island in the Mediterranean, off the 'toe' of Italy

Bohemia Here the King of Bohemia. It is common in Shakespeare's plays to find the name of a country for the king of that country.

visitation Official visit

justly Rightly, properly

entertainment i.e. provision for *his* entertainment

Beseech i.e. I beseech

freedom of my knowledge As one knowing the truth

unintelligent of our insufficience Unaware of our insufficiency.

You pay ... freely i.e. we do not need any return for our sincere friendship

Sicilia i.e. the King of Sicily (See note on 'Bohemia', above.)

over-kind Too kind

rooted The grammatical subject is 'affection'.

which As

branch Carrying on the metaphor in 'rooted'

encounters Meetings (not necessarily in conflict)

royally attorneyed Conducted in royal fashion by
representatives

vast Expanse (of sea)

continue i.e. may they continue

matter i.e. real reason, as opposed to 'malice' – unworthy
reason

of i.e. in

into my note Under my observation

physics the subject i.e. acts as a tonic on the king's subjects

Act I Scene 2

This long scene falls into three distinct sections, covered by
the three paragraphs below.

After Leontes has failed to persuade Polixenes to stay longer
as his guest, Hermione, his queen, succeeds. This gives rise to
Leontes' senseless suspicion that Hermione and Polixenes are
having a secret love-affair, notwithstanding that Hermione
induced Polixenes to stay at her husband's request.

Leontes speaks his mind to his old counsellor Camillo, and
will not be dissuaded from his suspicion by him, and orders
Camillo to poison Polixenes.

Instead, Camillo reveals the plot to Polixenes, who himself
has noted the King's black looks, and the two arrange to flee
from the country at once.

watery star i.e. moon. 'Watery' because it controls the tides.

note See note on 'into my note', above

Without a burden i.e. empty

cipher ... it Nought which multiplies the figures before it (by
ten), and so, although it signifies nothing by itself, with the others
it stands 'in rich place'. i.e. I say one 'We thank you', but it is
like a '1' followed by many '0's (as in the number 10,000).
These '0's by themselves are nothing, but following the '1' they
stand 'in rich place'. 'Moe' = more.

part Depart

question'd Given anxiety

upon Owing to

that i.e. I hope that there

sneaping Nipping (like a cold wind in early summer)

This i.e. my fears

Than ... to't Than to be affected by any test to which you can put us

Very sooth In good truth

part Divide. Not the same meaning as above. Leontes means that as Polixenes will not stay a week longer, they will compromise at three or four days, that is half a week.

's Us

I'll no gainsaying I will not be withstood.

Were ... it Were it essential to you that I granted your request, even although I considered it necessary to refuse it.

even Simply, just – i.e. that is all there is in it

which ... me And if you hinder my return your affection will do me harm

charge Burden, 'trouble'

Charge exhort. Not the same meaning as in the previous note.

by-gone day i.e. news of yesterday

ward Guard. A metaphor from fencing, meaning that he has lost his most telling argument.

But Only

adventure the borrow Chance, risk the borrowing, i.e. he will overstep his time by that amount. This is spoken to Polixenes.

let him i.e. let him stay (though this is not the literal meaning)

gest Date

good deed *In* good deed, or, as we now say, 'indeed'

jar Tick

What lady she Any lady whatever

limber Slight

your fees In those days prisoners who were able had to pay for their keep while in prison before they were released.

import offending Imply an offence (on my part)

lordings Little lords

chang'd Exchanged

blood i.e. passions

the imposition clear'd hereditary ours i.e. having cleared ourselves (even) of punishment for original sin which we inherit.

tripp'd i.e. tripped up, fallen

to boot Come (as well) to help me

of this make On account of this come to

answer i.e. answer for

that If

At ... not This, of course, is spoken to himself.

's Us, i.e. womenfolk

tongueless i.e. unpraised

Slaughters i.e. prevents

beat Run over. The general meaning of the passage is that you may lead us but not drive us.

goal Point

long i.e. long to know

clap i.e. signify by clasping hands

tremor cordis Palpitation of the heart

entertainment Reception, as we talk of 'entertaining' guests

free Open

derive a liberty Speak out freely

fertile bosom A generous disposition

padding Toying with

mort Death, referring to the notes sounded on the hunter's horn to proclaim the death of the deer

brows Referring to the horns supposed to grow on the brows of a cuckold, a man whose wife is unfaithful. This was a popular subject of Elizabethan cartoons and is frequently alluded to in contemporary plays.

I' fecks In faith

bawcock Fine fellow (Fr. *beau coq*). A rough term of endearment.

smutch'd Smudged

neat Remembering that 'neat' is also a word for cattle (who bear horns) he changes the word to 'cleanly'.

virginalling Playing with her fingers as if on a virginal, a stringed musical instrument with strings arranged something like those in a piano. Virginals became very popular in the first half of the seventeenth century.

pash Head

shoots i.e. horns

full Fully, entirely

o'er-dyed blacks Mourning clothes made by dyeing other garments (for the sake of economy)

As dice ... mine As a trickster who fixes no boundary between his property and mine (i.e. makes no distinction between them) would like dice to be

welkin i.e. sky-blue

villain Said in fun, of course, much as we call a child a 'little villain'.

Most dear'st In Elizabethan English a double superlative intensified the idea.

collop *lit.* slice of meat, but Leontes is referring to a contemporary proverb, 'It is a dear collop that is cut out of my own flesh'.

Affection A stronger word than now – 'love' or 'passion'.

centre i.e. centre of our being

not so held i.e. believed impossible

Communicat'st with dreams i.e. makes dreams seem true

this The supposed affair between Hermione and Polixenes, as in line 137. Leontes is not referring to his thoughts on 'affection'.

With ... art *lit.* you ('affection') act together with unreal things, i.e. make unreal things come true

fellow'st nothing Take unrealities for a companion

credent Believable

something As opposed to 'nothing'. The thought is that if love can act upon insubstantial things it can act upon a real person (like Hermione).

commission What should lawfully be allowed

hardening of my brows See note on 'brows', (p.37). Here 'brows' is in antithesis to 'brains' – Leontes' mind and body are affected by what he has seen.

Sicilia i.e. the King of Sicily

its An unusual word in Shakespeare, and one found only in his latest plays, showing that the word was just coming into use.
In the earlier and middle plays the neuter (as well as the masculine) possessive adjective is 'his'. 'Its' does not occur in the Authorized Version of the Bible (1611).

pastime Object of ridicule

methoughts The same as 'methought' (it seemed to me) later in the speech, probably by analogy with 'methinks'.

squash Unripe pea-pod

take eggs for money A term meaning 'brook an insult'. The literal meaning is to take something of little value instead of due payment.

happy man be's dole May his share in life be that of a happy man

If i.e. if I am

matter Interest, not the meaning on p.35.

December i.e. a day in December

childness Childishness

thick Thicken

So stands ... me This squire (*lit.* the attendant of a knight) does the same for me

cheap i.e. cheap to (provided freely for) him

Apparent to my heart Heir-apparent to my heart, i.e. he has the chief claim on my affection

shall's attend Shall we (*lit.* us) wait for

I am angling i.e. by giving you an opportunity to be in each other's company I am trying to catch you

neb Mouth, 'bill'. Leontes' jealous nature imagines that Hermione lifts her head towards Polixenes in a desire to kiss him.

allowing Approving

Gone already! From what follows it is evident that there is more in this remark than 'They are gone into the garden'. Leontes obviously means (or couples with it the meaning) 'My wife has gone', i.e. I have lost her affection.

a fork'd one i.e. horns. See note on 'brows', p.37.

Play Leontes uses the word here in the stage sense of playing 'a part'. The metaphor is continued in 'hiss me', as an actor is hissed off the stage.

whose issue The result of which (with a pun on 'issue')

cuckolds Husbands of unfaithful wives

shameless planet Referring to the planet Venus. (In classical mythology Venus was the Roman goddess of love.)

predominant In the ascendant, i.e. at its period of greatest influence over human lives. It was a widespread superstition of

Elizabethan times that men's natures and actions were influenced
by the stars, indeed, that a man's whole nature was influenced by
the star under which he was born.

thou'rt an honest man Spoken to Camillo

came home i.e. would not hold, dragged

material Important

They're here with me As we say, 'They've got me fixed'.

rounding 'Whispering'

gust Taste, i.e. hear of it

so it is As it happens

taken i.e. understood

thy conceit ... blocks Your imagination (like a sponge) will
take in (absorb) more than that of the common blockheads.
Notice how Leontes uses 'thy' to Camillo, but Camillo addresses
Leontes as 'you'. Similarly, later on in the scene, Polixenes
addresses Camillo as 'thou', but Camillo replies with 'you'.
'Thou' was the address from masters to servants or between close
companions. The monarchs and Hermione address one another
as 'you'. When Camillo is helping Florizel to escape (Act IV
Scene 3) he talks to Florizel as 'you' but Autolycus as 'thou'.
At the end of Act V Scene 2 the Clown, in his accession of fortune
considering himself the equal of Princes, addresses Autolycus as
'thou'.

But of Except by

severals Individuals, *lit.* separate people, implying there were few

lower messes People of lower rank, who sat at a lower place
('below the salt') at the common dining-table in the halls of
great houses

purblind Totally blind

chamber-councils Affairs of my private life. Some editors read
'counsels'.

we The royal 'we', singular in meaning

bide Dwell. Leontes repeats his charge.

that way i.e. towards honesty

hoxes Houghs, hamstrings

grafted in my serious trust Sharer in my most confidential
affairs. A metaphor from grafting the shoot of one plant on
another.

home To the end

drawn i.e. won (at the end of the game)

free i.e. from blame

puts forth Asserts itself. The verb is singular as 'negligence, folly and fear' are combined in a single idea. There are other similar instances. It was quite a common Elizabethan usage, and conversely we find a plural verb with a subject-word in the singular but whose idea is plural.

industriously Purposely

weighing Considering

Whereof ... non-performance The result of which condemned my not doing it, i.e. the result, when it was done, was a good one

that As

you Here the king comes closer and speaks to Camillo as a friend. He has something very secret to impart. Therefore he addresses him as 'you'. Camillo, too, is usually represented as an older man than Leontes.

your eye-glass The pupil of your eye

slipper i.e. not steadily faithful

hobby-horse Slang Elizabethan term for a loose woman

flax-wench i.e. girl flax-worker

'shrew Beshrew, curse

clouded i.e. blackened

present Immediate

which to ... true Which to repeat would be a sin as great as that (of which you accuse her) even though it were true

note Sign

honesty Chastity

pin and web Cataract of the eye, the 'pin' being the bright speck and the 'web' the film over it

Bohemia i.e. the King of Bohemia

Say it be Suppose

thou See note on 'you', above, and observe the contempt in this 'thou' after 'you lie, you lie'.

hovering Shifty, wavering (out for his own advantage)

liver i.e. body. In Shakespeare's time the liver was considered the seat of the affections (as the heart is now).

life i.e. mind and soul

glass i.e. hour glass

like her medal i.e. as if she were a medallion. (Leontes is evidently thinking of one with a portrait upon it.)

thrifts Interests

undo more doing Make any other action unnecessary. Or Leontes may mean 'prevent further relations between them'. In either case the phrase is a euphemism for Polixenes' murder.

form Position

bench'd Raised to a higher position. cf. note on 'lower messes', p.40.

worship A position of honour (Not a verb)

wink Closing of the eyes (not just for a moment)

rash i.e. swift in its action

Maliciously Malignantly. It is evident that Camillo means also 'with visible effect'.

crack Flaw

dread Revered

sovereignly being honourable Supreme in honour, *lit.* of sovereign honour

thee The pronoun is unusual from a subject to his sovereign. Camillo is reciprocating the king's show of affection (see note on 'you', p.41) and is, indeed, as a wiser, and older man, about to plead with him to change his mind. Later in the scene Polixenes says he will respect Camillo 'as a father', which again indicates that Camillo is represented as an elderly man.

Make that thy question Call that (my queen's dishonour) in question

muddy Dim

appoint Dress, array (i.e. to make it up when it does not really exist)

goads, thorns Each of these words bears the stress. Leontes says each slowly and deliberately

ripe moving Full evidence to move me

blench Turn aside (from the right path)

fetch off A euphemism comparable to those of Leontes

thereby ... tongues To stop scandal

poisoner No euphemism is necessary now Leontes has gone.

ground Justification

in rebellion with False to

so i.e. false to themselves

To do If I do

nor ... not In Elizabethan English a double negative intensifies the idea instead of logically cancelling it out.

Let villany itself forswear 't i.e. in its own interests

Happy star reign now! cf. note on 'predominant', p.39. He prays for good fortune now as an opportunity for an interview with Polixenes has just presented itself.

warp *lit.* become twisted

None rare Nothing out of the ordinary

As as if

Wafting ... contempt Turning away his eyes and letting his lip fall as a mark of contempt

breeding Equivalent to our metaphors 'brewing', or 'blowing up'

intelligent Intelligible

thereabouts Something like that (that you know and dare not tell)

you must i.e. you must explain

complexions Feelings (as shown in your looks)

be a party in Take part, or have a part in it. In this sentence Polixenes says that their change of feeling towards him will reciprocally alter his feelings to them.

distemper A pun on the two meanings, ill temper and ill health

basilisk Fabulous snake able to kill all on whom it looked

sped Fared, succeeded, got on

By On account of

gentleman In Elizabethan times the word referred to his rank, not his manners

Clerk-like experienced With a scholar's experience

gentry Nobility of rank, cf. 'gentleman'.

In ... gentle Our succession from whom gives us our rank (as gentlemen)

ignorant i.e. feigning ignorance

parts Qualities, as in the phrase 'a man of many *parts*'

this suit i.e. the granting of this suit

incidency Occurrence

if to be If it can be prevented at all. cf. note on 'To do', p.43.

me Instead of 'I', probably for emphasis

him By him

vice Screw (as in a vice)

his ... Best i.e. Judas Iscariot, who betrayed Christ

savour Referring to the popular notion that 'infection' can be smelt out

heard or read i.e. heard of or read about

Swear his thoughts over by Try to remove his ideas by invoking

influences See note on 'predominant', p.39.

you ... moon It is interesting to compare this passage with some well-known lines in *The Merchant of Venice*

> You may as well forbid the mountain pines
> To wag their high tops, and to make no noise
> When they are fretten with the gusts of heaven
> (Act IV Scene 1 lines 75–77)

or ... or Either ... or, a common Elizabethan usage

The standing of his body As long as his body stands

grow Have arisen

trunk Body

impawn'd As a pledge (of my honesty). Camillo is saying that he will accompany the King (of Bohemia), and so if the King finds him false it will be easy for him to take revenge.

whisper to Speak to in whispers about

several posterns Separate small gates (*lit.* back gates). In his next speech Camillo explains how he will be able to do what he says.

discovery Disclosure (to you)

seek to prove i.e. by reference to Leontes

thereon his execution sworn Once he has sworn to carry it (your murder) out, i.e. whatever he says to you, he will do it

thy places shall still neighbour mine The positions you occupy will always be near to mine (i.e. next in rank to those of the king)

hence From here (archaic)

jealousy Malice, envy

Profess'd Made profession of friendship

o'ershades Overshadows

Good ... suspicion May good speed help me, and comfort the
gracious queen, who (together with me) is the subject of this
attack, but is in no wise guilty of his ill-founded suspicion. His
speedy departure, he thinks, will comfort the queen by appeasing
her husband's anger.

avoid Depart

please May it please

take the urgent hour Remember that time is pressing

Revision Questions on Act I

1 What is the dramatic reason for stressing the friendship
between Leontes and Polixenes in Scene 1?

2 'Leontes is a study in self-generated jealousy'. Discuss this
remark in the light of Scene 2.

3 What part is played by Camillo in this Act?

Act II Scene 1

The prattle of the boy Mamillius with the ladies of the court
and with his mother the Queen is sternly interrupted by
Leontes and his Lords. Leontes has just heard of the flight of
Camillo and Polixenes, which he interprets as confirmation
of his suspicions of Hermione, and he openly accuses her of
adultery with Polixenes and consigns her to prison. In answer
to the reasonable protests of his Lords he curtly tells them to
mind their own business, but he does inform them that he has
sent to Apollo's temple 'for a greater confirmation', not because he is in any doubt of the result, but in order to satisfy
public clamour.

yet black ... best In Shakespeare's time blondes were
considered more beautiful, as Queen Elizabeth I was
sandy-haired.

so Provided

rounds i.e. gets bigger

wanton Play (with us instead of your mother)

A sad tale's best for winter Clearly this is the origin of the
title of the play.

crickets i.e. the ladies-in-waiting. Their chatter reminds the boy
of the chirping of crickets.

train Retinue, attendants

just censure Good judgement, 'true opinion'

Alack, for lesser knowledge Would that I knew less

blest i.e. blest with the knowledge I have

spider Popularly supposed to be venomous, but *only when it was
seen!*

hefts Heavings

discover'd Revealed, disclosed, *un*covered. cf. 'discovery', see
note p.44.

pinch'd Tricked, outwitted

trick Plaything

play Play with

than so Than when it has been done so

thee The very pronoun expresses his contempt. See note on
'thy conceit . . . blocks', p.40, and cf. 'thou thing', line 82.

I'd say Hermione says 'I *would* say' (and not, 'I say') because
she has not grasped yet that Leontes is seriously accusing her.

lean to the nayward Incline to the contrary view

without-door form Outward appearance

The shrug . . . brands The shrug of the shoulders, or the
disapproving cough of those who hear Hermione praised and are
jealous; they damn her by their faint praise.

out Wrong

That mercy . . . itself i.e. when Hermione's without-door form
is praised it would be merciful to pass by the praise with a shrug
of the shoulders or a cough, instead of revealing what she really
is. Slanderers brand virtuous people, but in the case of Hermione
passing it over (with a shrug or a cough) would be mercifully
hiding her guilt.

replenish'd Complete, thorough

a creature of thy place What you really are

barbarism The common people – abstract for concrete, as often in Elizabethan English. cf. 'calumny', 'mercy', and 'virtue' in Leontes' previous speech.

like Similar

degrees Ranks

mannerly distinguishment Distinction demanded by good manners

federary Confederate, accomplice

But Except

principal Accomplice, 'federary' (meaning here Polixenes)

bed-swerver One who turns away from her marriage bed (implying that she does so in order to share the bed of another)

That vulgars To whom common people

throughly Thoroughly

to say By saying

centre i.e. earth, supposed to be the centre of the universe in Shakespeare's time

afar off Indirectly, in some slight degree

But that Simply because

There's some ill planet reigns See note on 'predominant', p.39.

want Lack

charities Loves, good feeling

Shall I be heard? The guards cannot believe their ears when told to take Hermione to prison, and have done nothing.

fools Innocents. It is a term of endearment, not of contempt

action Charge

keep ... wife i.e. treat her as a horse (or a dog)

in couples i.e. lashed in couples like dogs, meaning, as explained in the next line, that he will feel he can trust Hermione no farther than he can see her

Than ... trust her The normal order would be, 'No further trust her than when I feel and see her'

abused Deceived

putter-on Instigator

land-damn Probably a Gloucestershire dialect word (hence not unfamiliar to a Warwickshire man) meaning 'proclaim his name through the village', as was done with scandalmongers in those days.

some five Some five years old

They'll pay for it Presumably meaning that they will be 'honour-flaw'd' too

doing When I do. Leontes obviously grips the hand of Antigonus, or perhaps strikes him.

see ... feel You see as well the instruments (my fingers or hand) that cause that feeling

lack I credit Do you not believe me?

lack i.e. lack 'credit'

ground Matter

follow our forceful instigation We (the royal 'we') should follow our strong provocation or incitement

Calls not Has no need of

or ... skill Either stupid or skilful enough to seem so. For 'or ... or', see note p.44.

overture Publicity

by Through, owing to

touch'd conjecture Roused (*lit.* reached) suspicion

nought for approbation Nothing lacking for proof

circumstances made up to Circumstantial evidence confirming

wild Rash

in post At express speed. 'Posts' were the places where fresh horses were stationed in Shakespeare's day.

Delphos, to Apollo's temple Delphi, in Boeotia, central Greece, had an oracle, which was much revered throughout the ancient world, to Apollo, god of music and the arts, and later of the sun. Shakespeare took the name from Greene (see p.2), who confused it with Delos, the island in the Aegean Sea where Apollo was born, and where there was a temple (but no oracle) to him. In Act III Scene 1 line 2 Delphos is called an 'isle', which plainly shows the error.

Of stuff'd sufficiency (Stuffed) fully of ability. A clumsy expression.

such ... truth Leontes no doubt looks at Antigonus here

From Away from

free Open to everyone

the treachery ... perform i.e. to murder him. He imagines that
  Polixenes planned to do to him what he planned to do to
  Polixenes.
raise Rouse

Act II Scene 2

Pauline, wife of Antigonus, is refused permission to see the
Queen in prison by her Gaoler, but is allowed to talk with
Emilia, her lady-in-waiting, in the Gaoler's presence. She is
informed that, owing to 'her frights and griefs', the Queen
has prematurely given birth to a daughter, but that the child
is doing well. Paulina offers to take the babe to show the King,
in the hope of softening his heart.

one who For 'one whom'
To ... commandment The normal order would be to put 'to
  the contrary' after 'commandment'
ado A to-do
honesty and honour Abstract for concrete again. See note on
  'barbarism', p.47 and cf. Act III Scene 2 lines 31–33 – 'innocence',
  'false accusation', 'tyranny', 'patience'.
gentle i.e. of noble ('gentle') birth. cf. notes on 'gentleman'
  and 'gentry', p.43.
put apart i.e. send away
Withdraw yourselves Spoken to her attendants
As passes colouring i.e. as black as possible. 'Passes' = surpasses.
on Upon, as a result of
Lusty Strong, vigorous
like Likely
lunes Fits of lunacy
red-look'd i.e. making me red in the face
free Freely-offered, generous
presently At once (the literal meaning)
hammered of i.e. was turning it over in her mind
tempt a minister of honour Try an honourable servant or
  agent

wit Good sense, wisdom
something nearer Probably into 'the next room' (see line 47)
pass it Let it pass
process (Legal) proceeding, carrying on the metaphor in 'law'
any i.e. any trespass there

Act II Scene 3

Leontes complains that he cannot sleep and is concerned for the boy Mamillius, who is declining, though the previous night the boy has had 'good rest'.

Paulina then comes before Leontes with Hermione's baby daughter, as arranged in the previous scene, but her uncompromising manner gets her nowhere, and Leontes has her thrown out: she leaves the child in the room with him. Leontes tells Antigonus (Paulina's husband) to have the baby burnt, but his Lords go down on their knees to him and he softens, and instead he orders Antigonus to abandon the child in 'some remote and desert place'.

At the end of the scene news is brought that the messengers who have been to Apollo's oracle have landed and, having made the journey in record time, are 'hasting to the court'.

Nor ... nor Neither ... nor – the usual Elizabethan usage. cf. note on 'or ... or', p.44.
harlot Vagabond, rascal. In this sense the word was applied to men in Shakespeare's day.
blank and level Aim and range. The 'blank' was the white spot in the centre of a shooting target.
she I can hook to me I can tackle her. The metaphor is from the grappling-irons thrown out by one ship to hold it to another.
moiety Fraction, small part (Fr. *moitié* = half)
is discharged Has left him
on't Of it
solely Alone
him i.e. Polixenes
Recoil Grammatically should be 'recoils', as the subject is 'thought', but the verb is attracted to the nearer noun 'revenges'.

This happens frequently in Shakespeare.

parties Allies, partners

present See note on 'presently', p.49.

be second to Help, as in a contest

free Innocent. Not the meaning of the word on p.41.

at him In to his presence

heavings 'Sighs'

humour Mood, disposition. cf. the title of Ben Jonson's play, *Every Man in his Humour*.

presses Keeps

gossips Sponsors at baptism

Commit me for committing honour Commit me to prison for doing an honourable deed. There is word-play on the two meanings of 'commit'.

La Pronounced 'law', still a vulgar exclamation of surprise. Akin to 'Lo!'

Less ... evils Appear less so (less obedient) in encouraging your evil course

by combat make her good By fighting a duel uphold her goodness

worst i.e. worst fighter

makes but trifles of his eyes Paulina is saying that she will scratch his eyes out

hand Lay hands on

mankind Forceful, masculine

intelligencing bawd Spying prostitute, one who carries intelligence, i.e. acts as go-between, in this case between Hermione and Polixenes

which ... honest i.e. the world has gone mad

Thou dotard Spoken to Antigonus

woman-tir'd, unroosted Hen-pecked (*lit.* torn, as a bird of prey tears flesh), knocked off your perch

dame Partlet The name of the hen in the story of *Reynard the Fox* (and also in Chaucer's *Nonnes Preestes Tale*) often applied to a managing wife in Shakespeare's day.

crone Old woman

by that forced baseness Under the base stigma of bastard which he has forced upon it

rotten i.e. as rotten

callat Prostitute

baits Vexes, teases, attacks, cf. the popular sport bull-*baiting*.

lay ... charge Apply the old proverb to you. Staunton quotes a reference to 'the old proverb' from Overbury's *Characters* ('A Sargeant', 1616), 'The devil calls him his white Sonne; hee is so like him that hee is the worse for it, and hee looks after [like] his father'.

trick Characteristic, trait

got Begot

yellow The colour associated with jealousy

not Not to be

lozel Worthless fellow, rogue, *lit.* one who has *lost* everything worth while

Once more Showing that, as when Leontes gave orders for Hermione to be taken to prison (Scene 1), the servants are slow to obey him

weak-hing'd Ill-balanced

Jove King of the Roman gods

these hands i.e. the hands of the servants who at length are pushing her out

encounter with Defy, challenge

proper Own

give us better credit Believe better of us, give us credit for something better

It shall not neither i.e. it shall not call me father either. Another double negative. See note on 'nor ... not', p.43.

Lady Margery Applied contemptuously to Paulina

this beard's gray Yet Leontes is under forty (twenty-three years older than Mamillius (see Act I Scene 2 lines 153–158)

adventure See note on 'adventure the borrow', p.36.

undergo Undertake

pawn Pledge. cf. note on 'impawn'd', p.44.

fail Failure

its See note p.38.

favour treatment, without our sense of *kindly* treatment

commend it strangely Commit it as a foreigner (being the daughter of Polixenes, a foreigner). 'Strangely' is here used in a somewhat different sense from the adjective 'strange' which precedes it.

ravens No doubt a Biblical reminiscence. See 1 Kings, 17, 4.

Wolves Shakespeare is no doubt thinking of Romulus (founder of Rome) and Remus, fabled to have been suckled by a wolf. He refers to the story in *Julius Caesar*.

offices Services

require Deserve

loss Be lost

posts Messengers. See note on 'in post', p.48.

Delphos See note p.48.

beyond account i.e. a record

Twenty-three days Such a realistic touch of circumstantial detail gives the truth of fact to fiction.

suddenly Quickly

session Court of justice. The word survives to-day in our 'Quarter *Sessions*'

just Honest, fair

Revision Questions on Act II

1 Describe the last meeting between Hermione and Mamillius.

2 What is (a) the ostensible, (b) the real reason that Leontes appeals to the oracle?

3 Is it surprising that Hermione considers Paulina a suitable person to take her infant child to Leontes in an effort to soften his heart?

Act III Scene 1

The two messengers from Apollo's oracle who, we were told at the end of the previous scene, have landed, are here talking about their impressions of their visit to the oracle, in 'a town in Sicilia', where, apparently, they have stopped to get 'fresh horses.' They bear the message of the oracle in a sealed package. It is evident that their sympathies are with the Queen, and this further enlists the sympathy of the audience for her.

This scene does nothing to advance the plot and is a scene of atmosphere only. It contrasts with the grim scenes on either side of it, like a shaft of sunlight between dark clouds, it relieves the tension of these harsh and noisy scenes – we feel we can relax for a few moments; finally, it increases our suspense, by keeping us waiting for the answer of the oracle.

isle Of Delphos. See note p.48.
common General, on every hand
caught Struck
habits Clothes, vestments
burst i.e. of utterance
Kin Akin
Jove See note p.52.
sense Senses
events Result, 'issue'
Apollo See note p.48, on Delphos.
carriage Management, ordering
clear or end Clear up or finish with – according as the result is good or bad
divine Priest

Act III Scene 2

At her trial (ordered by Leontes at the end of Act II Scene 3) Hermione defends herself with dignity, saying that defence of her honour, not preservation of her life, is her only concern. Ultimately she appeals to Apollo, whereupon the messengers from Apollo's oracle are admitted.

The oracle upholds Hermione's innocence and states that 'the king shall live without an heir, if that which is lost be not found!' At this Leontes exclaims

> There is no truth at all i' the oracle:
> The sessions shall proceed: this is mere falsehood.

Thereupon comes news that Mamillius is dead. At this dramatic proof of the last prophecy of the oracle Leontes gives way and sees things in their true light. Meanwhile Hermione has swooned at the news of her son's death. She is taken out, and soon Paulina returns to say that she also is dead, branding Leontes as the tyrant who has caused her death. Leontes goes out to see the bodies of his wife and son, vowing to visit their tombs every day for the rest of his life.

sessions See note 53.
Even pushes 'gainst our heart i.e. we are loth to hold this court, it goes against our better feelings
purgation Acquittal
pretence Plan, design, plot
circumstances See note on 'circumstances made up to', p.48.
laid open Revealed
but Only
The Testimony ... myself i.e. I have no witnesses
boot Help, assist. cf. note on 'to boot', p.37.
which ... pattern i.e. history has no precedent for my unhappiness.
take Bewitch, charm, cast a spell over, i.e. in a play
which owe Who own
For life ... spare As for life, I value it as I do grief (that is all life will mean to be in future), which I would do without
'T is ... for i.e. my child shares in my honour (or dishonour), and that is all I stand for. Hermione is not concerned with saving her life, but she is concerned with saving her honour.
uncurrent Improper
strain'd Gone too far
bound Boundary, limit
Less We should say 'more'. The construction is another example of the double negative. See note on 'nor ... not', p.43.
due Applicable
More ... fault Myself to be guilty of more than ordinary faults
he requir'd i.e. was his due
dish'd Dished up

how i.e. how it tastes

Wotting Knowing, i.e. if they know

dreams Fancies

Which The antecedent is 'my life'

of your fact Of your deed, i.e. who do what you have done

so past So are you past

concerns more than avails Gives you unavailing trouble

like to itself i.e. the proper treatment for an illegitimate child

which Referring to 'no father owning it'

easiest i.e. most merciful

bug Bogey, bugbear

commodity Advantage

give lost Count lost, give up as lost

like As if he were

starr'd Fated. See note on 'predominant', p.39.

post Notice-board. A post was usually fixed outside a sheriff's house for the display of official notices, proclamations, etc., corresponding to the notice-board outside a police-station to-day.

strumpet Prostitute

immodest Immoderate

'longs Belongs

fashion Kinds (whatever their rank)

of limit Sufficient

no life i.e. I am not pleading for my life

free i.e. from blame

The emperor of Russia In Greene (see p.2) it was the wife of Polixenes, not Leontes, who was the daughter of the Emperor of Russia.

flatness Completeness. cf. our phrase 'a *flat* denial', or 'That's *flat*'.

to report For reporting

with mere conceit Out of sheer imagination

speed Fortune, what may happen to her

My great ... oracle! In his speech immediately before the Servant rushed in

New Anew

minister Agent

tardied my swift command Delayed the execution of my

command for swift action

Not ... done i.e. death if he did not do it and a reward if he did it

Unclasp'd my practice Disclosed my plot

No richer than his honour His only riches consisting in his honour

glisters Glistens

Woe the while Alas for the present age

most worst Double superlatives (and comparatives) were common for emphasis in Elizabethan English

green and idle Childish and foolish

spices Smacks, sample bits

of a fool Like a fool

standing by i.e. to be revealed, ready to come forward

water i.e. tears

answer Charge, i.e. for you to answer

Tincture ... eye i.e. colour in her lip or sparkle in her eye

repent i.e. do penance for

stir Remove

still 'Perpetual'

receive affliction Afflict yourself. She withdraws the despair she laid upon him in her previous speech.

minded Reminded

fool i.e. I am a fool

remember Remind. The same meaning as 'minded', above.

take your patience to you i.e. comfort yourself with patience

upon them i.e. upon their memorial or monument

recreation Perhaps the literal meaning – re-creation, or perhaps he means that his only leisure pursuit will be the shedding of tears there.

with Under

exercise Religious duty. In Presbyterian circles prayers are still called 'devotional exercises'.

Act III Scene 3

In 'a desert country near the sea' in Bohemia, Antigonus leaves Hermione's child Perdita, as ordered by Leontes at the

Notes 53

end of Act II Scene 3. By the side of the child he leaves indications of her rank and a casket of gold, which may encourage the finder to look after her and bring her up. He is about to leave her and go to rejoin his ship, when he is chased off by a hunted bear.

An old shepherd comes along and finds Perdita. He halloos his son, who tells him how he has seen the ship near the shore swallowed up by the waves and Antigonus mauled and half-eaten by a bear. Father and son agree that the child has been left by fairies, and that the gold with her is 'fairy gold' and must be kept secret. The shepherd takes home the child and the gold, and his son goes off to bury what is left of Antigonus.

A ... sea Bohemia, of course, has neither deserts nor sea-board. See p.6.

art perfect Knowest for a fact

loud i.e. stormy

keep Live

some another Sometimes or the other

vessel ... fill'd Creature so sorrowful as this. The metaphor is obvious.

becoming i.e. in her sorrow

Perdita Latin for 'lost girl'

toys Trifles

squar'd Ruled

right True

character Handwriting (telling who she is)

these The 'bearing-cloth' and gold found later in the Scene by the Shepherd and the Clown

both ... thine i.e. seeing that the child was of some consequence the finder might bring it up for nothing (in hope of reward or advancement) without spending the gold. 'Pretty' = pretty one, 'still' = always (cf. note p.57).

Weep I cannot Referring to the injunction in his dream. See line 32.

savage clamour i.e. the noise of the huntsmen and hounds

chase Hunted animal

I am gone for ever! In view of the prophecy in his dream. See
  lines 34–36.

Exit, pursued by a bear 'If anyone ask my private opinion why
  the bear came on, it is that the Bear-pit in Southwark, hard by
  the Globe Theatre, had a tame animal to let out, and the Globe
  management took the opportunity to make a popular hit'. Sir
  Arthur Quiller-Couch in *Shakespeare's Workmanship* (p.238,
  C.U.P.).

ancientry Old people

boiled brains As we say, 'hot-heads'

an If

barne Child. cf. Scots 'bairn'.

child i.e. girl-child. The word is still so used in country dialects.

scape Escapade

stair i.e. backstair

takes up Submerges

yest i.e. foam

land-service A military term, as opposed to naval service (the
  Clown has just been talking of the ship), used here for a
  humorous description of Antigonus

flap-dragon'd Swallowed – as a drinker swallows a flap-dragon
  (raisin in a drink)

old The Shepherd had not been told by the Clown that the
  man was old, but it is a natural assumption, and in any case the
  word need not be pressed too far.

ship-side i.e. ship's side. The *'s* is often omitted by Shakespeare
  before another *s*

Heavy i.e. sorrowful

bearing-cloth The cloth in which a child was wrapped to be
  taken to baptism. It was often costly and was handed down in
  families from generation to generation.

changeling A child left by the fairies in exchange for another.
  Here, obviously, it means one taken by the fairies and abandoned.

well to live Well-to-do

up with 't i.e. pick it up

close Secret. 'Fairy gold' (i.e. gold left by the fairies) was
  supposed to turn to ashes if it was not kept secret. A very
  convenient supersition for finders of lost property!

next Nearest
Let my sheep go i.e. do not bother about my sheep
curst Bad-tempered. The Clown implies that it is safe to go
  near the place where the bear was, because now the animal has
  had a meal he will not be ferocious.
on't Out of it, as a result of it, because of it

Revision Questions on Act III

1 Comment on the fairness of Hermione's trial, even sup-
posing the charge to have some foundation.

2 Describe Leontes' first reaction to the vindication of Hermione by the oracle and say what modified it.

3 'The tearing of Antigonus by the bear is the most ludicrous
incident in Shakespeare' (p.7). What is *your* opinion?

Act IV Prologue (or Scene 1)

Time enters to take us to sixteen years later, during which
Leontes has shut himself up in his grief and Perdita has grown
up in Bohemia a wondrously charming girl.
  Comments on the style of this scene will be found on page 5.
  In some editions of the play the Prologue is called Scene 1
(of Act IV), hence the alternative numbering of scenes in
this Act.

try Test
joy ... bad i.e. joy of good and terror of bad
that makes and unfolds error Who cause and clear up
  mistakes. The verb in the third person singular makes it appear
  as if Time is being described instead of speaking himself. It is,
  however, not uncommon after a relative pronoun in Elizabethan
  English.
growth untried Progress of events unexamined
one self-born One which I have created myself
plant and o'erwhelm custom Create and destroy a custom

The same ... receiv'd For what I always have been, since
  before the ancient or the modern world
them i.e. the old order
seems to i.e. seems stale compared to. The story of Perdita
  now seems bygone history ('stale'), but in due course things that
  are fresh in the news to-day will similarly become 'stale'.
As As if
Leontes leaving i.e. I leaving Leontes. But 'grieving' refers to
  Leontes.
fond jealousies Foolish suspicions
the king Polixenes. His son was mentioned in Act I Scene 2
  lines 164–171.
pace I pace
Equal with wondering Equal to the wonder it aroused
list not Do not wish to
to her adheres Concerns her
argument Subject, theme. The 'news' which Time 'brings forth'.
Of this allow i.e. allow me to do this
If ever ... now i.e. in the theatre
that Allow, admit that

Act IV Scene 1 (or 2)

Camillo, still at the palace of Polixenes, is homesick and asks
permission 'to lay his bones' in his own country, especially
as the penitent Leontes has sent for him. Polixenes urges him
to stay, as a valued counsellor and friend, and goes on to seek
his help in finding out why the young Prince Florizel is 'of
late much retired from court', reported by the King's in-
formers to be resorting to the cottage of a shepherd with a
lovely daughter, a shepherd who has grown unspeakably rich.
Polixenes asks Camillo to 'lay aside the thoughts of Sicilia'
and accompany him to the shepherd's cottage in disguise.

The conversation about the new characters, Florizel and
Perdita, who belong to the second half of the play, arouses
our interest in them and heightens the suspense. The effect

is the same as when, in Act I, Scene 1, Camillo and Archidamus talk about Leontes and Polixenes. This method is thoroughly Shakespearean (see p.7).

The use of prose in the scene is discussed on page 27.

't is a sickness i.e. it hurts me

fifteen Camillo's slight error (see Act IV Prologue line 6) in speaking from memory is natural and adds to the reality of the impression

aired Out and about

allay Means of allaying, comfort

o'erween Am presumptious enough, *lit.* 'overthink'

without Other than

heaping friendship The increasing of my friendship with you

brother i.e. brother king

gracious Pleasing. Perdita is said to be 'grown in grace', Act IV Prologue line 24.

approved Proved

missingly i.e. from his absence

is less frequent i.e. applies himself less frequently

look upon his removedness i.e. spy on what he is doing when he is away

from i.e. away from

estate Property, not necessarily landed property, as we use the word of the property left by a deceased person

is extended Reaches proportions

intelligence Information, as in the phrase 'Intelligence Service'

but The use of this word seems to indicate that the trend of Polixenes' thought is, 'Whatever good fortune this information may mean to anyone else, yet I fear that it is the attraction which draws our son there'.

angle Bait, *lit.* fishing hook, now surviving in the verb and the derivative 'angler'

Act IV Scene 2 (or 3)

We are introduced to a vagabond rogue, Autolycus, who comes singing his way on in merry mood. He picks the Clown's pocket, learns from him of a sheep-shearing feast to be held, and determines to be there to see what he can get out of the other shepherds.

peer Appear

doxy Mistress (slang)

in Instead of

pale Pallor, pale faces – in antithesis to 'red blood'

pugging Thieving, corresponding to our slang word 'pinching'

a quart of ale What he could buy with the money obtained from selling the stolen white sheet

aunts Another slang word for 'mistresses', like 'doxy' above

three-pile Three-piled velvet, i.e. thick, rich velvet, worn when he was in court service

budget Wallet or haversack in which a tinker carried the tools of his trade

my ... give I may well confess what I am (a thief).

avouch Affirm, declare

when ... linen i.e. the kite may steal 'lesser linen' to build its nest, but I steal only sheets (hung out on hedges to dry). 'Look to' = look after.

litter'd under Mercury Born when the planet Mercury was 'predominant' or in the ascendant. In Latin mythology, Mercury was the patron god of thieves (among others). He had a son Autolycus, who inherited this part of his father's nature.

unconsidered Not properly looked after

With die and drab Through dice and women

purchas'd i.e. came by

caparison, dress Properly fine equipment, but used sarcastically by Autolycus as he looks down on his rags

my revenue is the silly cheat I get my money out of simple people

knock Being knocked down (for highway robbery)

the life to come Probably Autolycus simply means the future in this world and is not thinking of the life to come in any other

sleep ... it i.e. do not worry about it

'leven wether tods Eleven sheep yield a tod (12.70 kg = 28lb) of wool

odd i.e. an odd 5p over the pound

springe Snare, trap

cock i.e. woodcock. The woodcock was a byword for stupidity.

me *lit.* for me, but really redundant and of no special
  significance. It was often used in free and easy speech.

three-man songmen Singers of three-part rounds, or 'catches'
  as they were called

means Tenors, *lit.* those who sing the middle ('mean') part

hornpipes i.e. hornpipe tunes

warden A kind of large cooking pear

note List, presumably mental list, since the Clown was illiterate

race Root

o' the sun i.e. dried in the sun

I' the name of me! A mild (and silly) oath, to avoid mentioning
  the name of God

a million Emphasis on the *a*, i.e. only *one* million strokes (let
  alone 'millions')

come to a great matter Mount up to a great many

footman i.e. pedestrian

You ... office The sarcasm of this is obvious, as Autolycus has
  picked the Clown's pocket

offer me no money Had the Clown done so, he would of course
  have discovered his loss

troll-my dames A game on a board, something like bagatelle
  (Fr. 'trou madame')

abide Trying to appear learned the Clown uses the word as if
  it meant 'make a short stay'. Really it means just the same as
  'stay'.

ape-bearer One who exhibited an ape (at fairs, etc.)

process-server Server of a summons, much the same as
  'bailiff'

compass'd ... Son Obtained a puppet show which mimicked
  the story of the Prodigal Son. Incidentally, this shows how drama
  from Bible subjects (the source of all popular drama in England)
  still survived in country districts in the time of Shakespeare.
  (See p.11).

in i.e. as a

prig Thief (slang). Not the meaning it has to-day.

pace softly Walk slowly
prove sheep i.e. turn out to be simpletons
unroll'd Struck off the roll (register – of thieves)
hent Hold (and therefore climb over)
sad Serious

Act IV Scene 3 (or 4)

Florizel and Perdita come to the Shepherd's cottage for the sheep-shearing festival (spoken of in the previous scene), Florizel disguised as a 'swain' (though Perdita knows who he is), Perdita dressed as 'mistress of the feast'. After Florizel has paid her pretty compliments, the other shepherds and shepherdesses come along, the old Shepherd bringing with him two visitors, Polixenes and Camillo, disguised, as planned between them in Scene 1, in order to investigate Florizel's activities. The festival starts, and Polixenes questions the Shepherd about the 'fair swain' who dances with his daughter, whom he cannot help but notice has a nobility of bearing beyond her place.

Thereupon a pedlar is announced, and Autolycus comes in and pushes his wares on the country lovers. The rough humour of this episode contrasts with the high romance of the love of Florizel and Perdita.

The festivities continue with 'a dance of twelve Satyrs'. Polixenes gets Florizel to talk of his love for Perdita, which he does gladly and avers that he wants to be 'contracted' to Perdita there and then. Polixenes questions Florizel about his father and says that a father should be consulted before his son's engagement. Florizel puts him off, whereupon Polixenes throws off his disguise, summons Florizel back to court, forbids him ever to meet Perdita again, threatens Perdita with a cruel death if Florizel is admitted to her house in future and suspends judgement on the Shepherd. He goes out; but after he has left, Florizel vows that his love comes before his throne and he will marry Perdita in defiance of his father. Camillo suggests to Florizel that he should take Perdita to King Leontes in Sicilia and pretend that he has come on a mission from his father; and he tells Florizel that he can vouch for his favourable reception. He arranges disguise for the lovers, Florizel exchanging clothes with Autolycus, who happens to be just by and gets better clothes *and* a gift of money for his services. Camillo's advice has an ulterior motive, however, for after Florizel has acted on it, he plans to tell Polixenes where he has gone, so that Polixenes will follow and tell Camillo to accompany him. Thus Camillo will be able to return to his beloved Sicilia.

Meanwhile, to save his life, the Shepherd resolves to tell the King that Perdita is none of his. He is going to the court with his evidence (the 'fardel' left with Perdita when she was abandoned as a child) when he meets Autolycus, dressed as a courtier after exchanging clothes with Florizel (but see note on 'Seest ... enfoldings,' p.75). Autolycus tries (unsuccessfully) to find out his business with the King, but, with an eye to profit, offers for a consideration to use his influence to give him an easy approach into the royal presence, but really he plans to bring him to the ship in which Florizel is setting sail, in order to help Florizel, who, he hopes, will give him more money. He thus schemes to get double gain from the one action.

weeds Clothes. Now used only in the phrase 'widow's weeds'.
Flora Roman goddess of flowers
in April's front At the beginning of April
petty i.e. lesser, as in 'Petty Sessions', 'petty officer', 'petty larceny', etc. (Fr. *petit*)
extremes These are explained in lines 7–10.
mark Centre of attention
swain's wearing Shepherd's dress
prank'd Dressed
mess Part of the table (higher and lower ranks). See note on 'lower messes', p.40.

Digest it with a custom i.e. are used to it

glass i.e. mirror

I bless ... ground This, of course, is to account for their meeting in a natural way

difference forges dread Difference (in rank) between us makes me afraid

your The emphatic word

bound up The metaphor is from book-binding

flaunts Finery

Jupiter became a bull According to Roman legend, Jupiter, king of the gods (also known as Jove), changed himself into a bull in order to win Europa as his bride. He met her on the seashore and carried her on his back over the waters to Crete, where he married her.

Neptune a ram Neptune, Roman god of the sea (hence 'green') and brother of Jupiter, carried off the beautiful princess Theophane to an island. As she was pursued there by her many suitors, he transformed her into a sheep and himself into a ram. Theophane gave birth to the golden-fleeced ram of Colchis (the fleece later carried away by Jason and the Argonauts).

Apollo See note on 'Delphos, to Apollo's temple', p.48. Here Apollo is thought of as the sun-god (hence 'fire-rob'd' and 'golden'). He became a shepherd in order to woo the nymph Daphne. She fled from him, however, and as he gained upon her she prayed to the gods for help and was changed into a laurel bush just as he caught up with her.

in a way With a purpose

I my life Probably she means that she will have to give up her life, not merely change her way of life and become a shepherdess again.

forc'd Far-fetched

gentle Gentle one

pantler Servant in charge of the pantry

On his shoulder i.e. at his shoulder to serve him

a feasted one i.e. one invited to the feast

to 's welcome Welcome to us

Seeming and savour Appearance and scent

Grace and remembrance Rue was for grace, and rosemary for remembrance. See *Hamlet*, Act IV. Scene 5: 'There's rosemary, that's for remembrance . . . There's rue for you . . . we may call it herb of grace o' Sundays'.

gillyvors Gillyflowers. In Shakespeare's time the name was applied to clove-scented pinks, not, as now, to wallflowers.

bastards Because they are crossed, not a pure variety. Hence they are 'streak'd'

slips Cuttings

an art The art of crossing two different varieties

piedness Different colours, 'streaks'

mean Means

makes that mean i.e. bestows the power of life and growth in the plant

we marry . . . stock Yet what Polixenes defends in nature he is soon to condemn when his son wishes to marry one of 'wildest stock'

painted Comparing herself to the flowers variegated in colour

Hot i.e. with a strong scent

savory A herb of the mint family

my fair'st friend She addresses Florizel

time of day i.e. time of life

Proserpina . . . wagon Proserpina, daughter of the goddess Ceres (corn), was picking flowers in Enna, in Sicily, when Dis (Pluto) carried her off to be his queen in the underworld. Ultimately she was allowed to return to the world for two-thirds of every year (corresponding to the growing season).

daffodils . . . beauty An oft quoted passage.

take Bewitch, charm

dim Of a soft colour

Juno Wife of Jupiter (see note p.67) and Queen of Heaven

Cytherea Venus, Roman goddess of love, born from the seafoam near the mountainous island of Cythera, south of Greece

prime-roses Primroses

Phoebus Another name for the sun-god Apollo. See note on 'Apollo', p.67.

crown imperial Yellow ('crown') fritillery

flower-de-luce Iris (Fr. *fleur-de-lis*)

these I lack Because it is not springtime

my sweet friend i.e. Florizel

quick Alive

Whitsun pastorals Whitsuntide country festivals where scenes from the lives of Robin Hood and Maid Marian were acted (combined with morris-dancing)

What ... done Whatever you do, you always do it in the best way possible.

for As for

each ... queens Each thing you do, so unique in every particular, makes your present actions supreme, so that all your acts are royal. Florizel is here only expanding his opening sentence in this speech.

large Liberal

fairly Becomingly

skill Reason

turtles Turtle-doves

blood look out Blush

good sooth In good truth

marry An oath by the Virgin Mary

garlic ... with i.e. try putting garlic in your mouth so that you do not notice her bad breath

manners i.e. best behaviour. In other words, 'Let us have no vulgar jokes here'.

worthy feeding Valuable pasture-land

like sooth Truthful. See note on 'good sooth', above.

another The other

featly Gracefully

light upon her i.e. win her as his bride

she shall ... of The Shepherd is probably referring to the riches found by her side when she was picked up as a baby.

tabor Small drum

tell Count

bawdry Vulgarity

burthens Refrains

dildos and fadings Words used in ballad refrains, an example of which follows

stretch-mouthed Dirty-mouthed

break ... matter Put in vulgar extempore material of his own

brave Fine

admirable Conceited, marvellously ingenious

unbraided Unsoiled, i.e. new, not second-hand

ribands Ribbons

points Tagged laces (acting as buttons), with a pun on the
  meaning 'legal po nts'

inkles Tapes

caddises Worsted laces or ribbons used for garters

sleeve-band Cuff

square The front of a dress, above the waist, usually covered
  with embroidery

of Some of

Cyprus Crape (first made in Cyprus)

Bugle Of black beads

necklace amber Amber beads for making a necklace

quoifs Caps

stomachers Embroidered front-pieces of dresses, covering the
  breast and the pit of the stomach, ending downwards in a point
  over a full skirt.

poking-sticks Rods used for setting ruffs after starching. They
  were heated in the fire and used hot.

be the bondage i.e. I shall have to pay for them.

against Ready for

plackets Petticoats

kiln-hole Fire-place used for making malt, a byword for a place
  of gossip

clamour Stop, silence

tawdry-lace A (cheap and) showy neckerchief. Originally one
  sold at the Fair of St Audrey in Ely (hence 'tawdry'). St Audrey
  (Etheldreda) was the patron saint of Ely Cathedral.

cozened Cheated. The literal meaning of 'cozen' is to cheat a
  man by pretending to be a 'cousin', a form of confidence trick.

charge Value

a-life On my life

a burthen One birth

carbonadoed Sliced up

wives Women (OE wif)

moe More

for Because
passing Surpassingly extremely
bear Sing
grange Farm-house
anon Immediately
utter Offer (for sale), as in 'uttering a (false) coin'
men of hair i.e. like Satyrs (the Servant's 'Saltiers'). Satyrs were classical woodland deities, half goat, half man. Dances of satyrs were often introduced in masques, which were getting very popular at the time *The Winter's Tale* was written. The two companion plays to *The Winter's Tale*, *Cymbeline* and *The Tempest*, both contain masques.

From a masked dance the masque had developed into a medley of dance, music, opera, pantomime, pageant and elaborate scenery. The patronage of James I increased its popularity, and it reached its hey-day at the end of his reign. It was generally written to order, and produced privately to grace a festive occasion in some important family, and the performers would be amateur actors among the guests. We know that *The Tempest* was performed at the Court of James I during the celebrations in honour of the betrothal of his daughter Elizabeth to the German Prince Frederick, Elector Palatine, in 1612, and it is possible that for this occasion the play in its original form was cut in order to introduce the masque which Prospero prepares to give his blessing to Miranda and Ferdinand – a typical wedding masque.

gallimaufry Hotch-potch, jumble
some ... bowling i.e. the aristocracy ('the gentlemen'), bowls being then an aristocratic game. Perhaps punning on the smoothness of a bowling green.
squier Foot-rule
O father ... hereafter This is the end of a conversation between Polixenes and the Shepherd, while the shepherds and the satyrs have been holding the stage.
handed Handled, i.e. was occupied with
she Lady
knacks Trinkets, knick-knacks.
marted Traded. ('Mart' = market.)

Interpretation should abuse Should interpret your action wrongly

bounty Generosity

straited Hard put to it, in hard straits

make ... her Take any thought for happy possession of her

looks Looks for, expects

O, hear me He now turns to Perdita.

Ethiopian Used loosely for any African negro

bolted Sifted

force Strength

speak Put it into words

By the pattern ... his Metaphor from dressmaking. She means that she measures the purity of his intentions by her own – a feminine intuition.

virtue Power

one being dead This is not likely to help his cause! There is much dramatic irony derived from Florizel's ignorance of his father's presence, of course.

Contract Bind in a marriage engagement

reasonable Demanding reason

altering rheums Rheumatism that changes (a person)

dispute his own estate Talk about his own affairs

being childish When he was a child

Something Somewhat

reason It is reasonable that

my son The dramatic irony here is not hidden from the speaker.

Divorce Separation (not in a matrimonial legal sense)

Discovering See note on 'discover'd', p.46.

affects Shows affection for

piece Paragon

of force Perforce

cop'st with Dost encounter

state Position

fond Foolish

That Because

knack Polixenes now uses contemptuously the word he used before in kindly fashion. (See note p.71.)

Far Farther

Deucalion Deucalion and his wife Pyrrha were the sole survivors of the Flood in Greek mythology. They repeopled the earth by casting stones which became men and women. Deucalion corresponds to Noah in Hebrew legend.

churl Peasant

dead Deadly, death-dealing

enchantment Spoken to Perdita

yea ... thee You are worthy of him too, since he makes himself so low as to be unworthy of you, except for his royal blood ('our honour').

undone Ruined

alike Indifferently

died i.e. died on

Where ... dust i.e. in an unsanctified ceremony

adventure Venture, risk

plucking Being plucked

not purpose Do not purpose

fancy Love

for all i.e. *not* for all

wombs i.e. hides within itself

passion Anger

Tug Tussle, have it out with one another

deliver i.e. deliver the news

Shall nothing benefit your knowledge Will be of no use for you to know

Purchase Obtain, gain

fraught with curious business Burdened with business full of care

as thought on As soon as he thinks about them

ponderous Weighty, important to you

receiving Reception

disjunction Separation

forefend Forbid

Your ... qualify Your angry (*lit.* discontented) father I will strive to pacify.

liking Agreement with it

But ... blows But as the unexpected event is responsible for what we do rashly, so we say that we are the slaves of chance.

and flies carried along by every wind that blows. For 'wildly' see note p.48.

list Listen

undergo Undertake

habited Dressed

free Welcoming. cf. note p.37.

divides ... kindness Is cleft between his (former) unkindness (to Polixenes) and his (present) kindness (to his son)

colour for my visitation Excuse for my visit

comforts Consolation, not individual comforts but comfort in general

sitting Interview

bosom Inmost thoughts

sap Hope

undream'd Undreamed of

one i.e. one misery

take in Overcome

these seven years i.e. for a very long time

as forward ... her birth i.e. as high in breeding as she is low in birth. Some editors read *our* birth'.

medicine Doctor, i.e. one who puts things right

furnish'd Equipped, 'appointed' (in Camillo's reply)

appear Appear so

pomander Perfumed ball

table-book Notebook. cf. the word 'tablet'.

in picture To look at

pettitoes Feet (*lit.* pig's feet – used humorously)

that ... ears They could only hear (they could not see or feel what I was doing)

pinch'd Stolen (slang). Slang alters rapidly, but this word has persisted to the present day.

geld a cod-piece i.e. rob (*lit.* cut off) a pocket. The 'cod-piece' was the name given to the hanging outside pocket worn with trunk hose.

whoo-bub Hubbub

choughs Crows

discase thee Undress yourself

pennyworth Bargain

some boot Some advantage, something extra. cf. 'to boot', note p.37. Camillo gives Autolycus some money, although the 'poor fellow' has the best of the bargain in any case.

dispatch Hurry up

flayed Stripped

earnest A pledge (of more to follow), a first instalment as it were

my prophecy i.e. that you are fortunate

Dismantle you Change your cloak

disliken ... seeming Disguise your real appearance

over i.e. looking out for you

undescried Unrecognized

review See again (the literal meaning)

clog A term of contempt for Perdita, *lit.* encumbrance. Autolycus thinks that Perdita is some undesirable girl Florizel has picked up.

brother-in-law The Shepherd is not very clear about family relationships.

fardel Bundle

excrement Excrescence; in this case a false beard

your worship The Shepherd addresses Autolycus thus as he is dressed in Florizel's clothes – the clothes of a gentleman of rank. But see note on 'His garments are rich', below.

condition Nature

having Property

they do not give The emphatic word is 'give' – they do not *give* us the lie, we pay them for it.

taken yourself with the manner Stopped yourself in the very act (of living). If Autolycus had not corrected his statement 'they often give us soldiers the lie', he would have told a lie.

Seest ... enfoldings Shakespeare has slipped up here. Florizel was not dressed as a courtier, but as 'a swain', ready for the festival. 'Enfoldings' = clothes. Autolycus is speaking in a stilted parody of courtly style.

toaze Tousle

cap-a-pe From head to foot (Fr. *cap à pied*)

Advocate's ... pheasant There is much parody of court affectations in all this conversation.

His garments are rich See note on 'Seest . . . enfoldings', above.

by the picking on's teeth At the time *The Winter's Tale* was
  written, toothpicks were coming into fashion among the
  aristocratic classes. cf. note on 'Advocate's . . . pheasant', above.

hand-fast Custody

germane Related. Autolycus is still talking in the 'grand style'.

aqua-vitae Whisky

prognostication Forecast. Autolycus is thinking of a long-term
  forecast in an almanac.

capital Deserving of death

being something gently considered For a reasonable
  consideration

tender Introduce

case Playing on the meaning 'body'

occasion Opportunity

which Refers to the second 'occasion' – a 'means to do the prince
  my master good'

back Out

shore them Put them ashore

Revision Questions on Act IV

1 Give a summary of Time's speech (Prologue) in your own
words.

2 Do you consider Polixenes' spying on his son justifiable?

3 Enumerate the wares which Autolycus brings to sell at the
sheep-shearing feast.

4 Point out the way that the humorous interludes in the
great pastoral scene (3) throw up the serious episodes.

5 Which character is the centre of attraction in this scene(3)?
Justify your opinion.

6 Divide this long scene into six separate sections.

Act V Scene 1

We return to the court of Leontes after sixteen years. His grief for Hermione shows no sign of abating and is aggravated by Paulina's taunts. Some people would have him wed again, to secure the succession; but he thinks no wife could compare with the one he has lost; and he agrees never to marry unless to a woman of Paulina's choice.

Thereupon Florizel and Perdita are announced, and while it appears strange they come so ill-attended, Florizel tells a plausible tale that satisfies Leontes, and he is made welcome. He introduces Perdita as his wife, a Libyan princess: everyone is struck by her beauty.

Then comes a messenger from Polixenes, newly come to the city with Camillo, requesting Leontes to arrest his son, and telling the reason why: Florizel realizes that Camillo has betrayed him. The messenger also says that Polixenes and Camillo have met the father and brother of the 'seeming lady' Florizel has run off with. These relations of Perdita have quitted their country with the prince, and are being held for questioning. Florizel appeals to Leontes for help: Leontes is not unwilling and defers action until he has seen Polixenes.

good now Please
done the time more benefit Been more useful
remembrance Continuance
fail Failure
Incertain i.e. they will be uncertain what to do in the absence of an appointed leader
well i.e. in heaven
Respecting Compared with
Will i.e. have determined to
shall i.e. shall be found
should ... be Modified from 'is', the definite statement which is what she really means
great Alexander Alexander the Great (356–323 BC), King of Macedonia (Greece), died young and without appointing an heir

to his vast dominions. After many insurrections his generals established his posthumous son and one of his half-brothers as joint kings, but his empire soon broke up.

like Likely

squared me to Lined up with, metaphor from a set square

No i.e. there are no. cf. 'we offenders', below.

'Why to me?' i.e. why this insult to me?

rift Split

Affront Confront

walk'd If walked

out of circumstance Unceremonious

visitation See note on 'colour for my visitation', p.74.

fram'd Arranged

thy grave i.e. you who are in your grave

professors else Who profess any other faith

who Those who

not women Paulina implies that women will not love one more beautiful than themselves

assisted with Attended by

He dies to me again i.e. I feel it all over again.

Unfurnish Deprive

print i.e. copy

Though ... him Though life means misery for me, I desire it in order to see him again

at friend In friendship

but Except that

worn times Old age

offices Compliments

Libya On the Mediterranean coast of North Africa, west of Egypt

climate here Sojourn in this region

graceful The literal meaning – full of grace. The word has a similar meaning to 'holy' and 'sacred'.

attach Arrest

amazedly Confusedly

becomes my marvel Suits my state of wonder

question Interrogation at law

divers deaths in death Death by a variety of tortures
The odds ... alike The odds are the same for (i.e. against)
those of high rank and for those of low rank.
worth Rank
visible Visibly
ow'd ... now i.e. were no older than I am
Your honour Provided that your honour be

Act V Scene 2

In this conversation of Gentlemen of the Court we learn that
the Shepherd's evidence has convinced Polixenes, and later
Leontes, of Perdita's identity. The two kings have met. The
Shepherd and the Clown, his son, have been rewarded; and
suddenly becoming a 'gentleman' goes to the Clown's head.

The Court has gone to see a statue of Hermione just finished
by a famous sculptor for Paulina.

For a consideration of the use of prose in this scene see p.27.

notes of admiration Signs of astonishment
the cases of their eyes Their eyelids
passion Great feeling (not necessarily love)
seeing What he saw
importance Import
were pregnant by circumstance Had come to light by
circumstantial evidence
countenance Behaviour, demeanour
favour Face, features
clipping Embracing
weather-bitten conduit Weather-beaten water-pipe.
Water-pipes were usually made of wood (elm) in Elizabethan
England, and the old Shepherd's wrinkled face would suggest the
comparison.
undoes description to do it i.e. beggars description
credit be asleep i.e. nobody believes it
Wrackt Wrecked
instruments i.e. the people

locks The change to the present tense makes the description more dramatic.

newly perform'd Just finished

Julio Romano Giulio Romano (1492–1546), an Italian painter (not sculptor) whose work was well known in artistic circles in England.

beguile Nature of her custom i.e. take away from Nature the customary admiration awarded her. The Third Gentleman means that people would give to the sculptor the admiration usually given to Nature.

ape Copy

piece Add to, increase

unthrifty to our knowledge i.e. not increasing our knowledge when we can

prince i.e. prince's ship

began to be much sea-sick A human touch

relished Found acceptance, or, as we say, 'gone down well'

moe More

denied Refused

this The

give me the lie Call me a liar

preposterous For 'prosperous'

an it like your good worship See note p.75. Now the tables are turned. The last time this phrase was used it was by the Clown to Autolycus (dressed in Florizel's clothes).

franklins Yeomen, small landholders

tall fellow of Bold fellow with

to my power As well as I can, to the best of my ability

picture See note on 'Julio Romano' above.

Act V Scene 3

At a Chapel in Paulina's house, Leontes, Polixenes, Florizel, Perdita and Camillo gather to see the statue of Hermione mentioned in the previous scene. It is really Hermione herself, and all stand amazed at the lifelike presentation, though Leontes notices added wrinkles. In due course Hermione descends from the pedestal where she has been standing motionless like a statue and embraces Leontes (without a word to him), but is more moved at seeing her grown-up daughter. Thus the play ends on a note of happy reunion, a mellow rather than a joyous happiness (see also page 21). Leontes, as he had agreed, has taken a wife found by Paulina, and in return he fixes up a (quite unnecessary) marriage between Paulina and Camillo.

the great ... thee There has been little evidence of it in the play! No doubt at the present juncture Leontes appreciates the fact that she has kept his grief green.

home In full. cf. note p.41.

We honour you with trouble i.e. (as king) I do you honour by coming to visit you and thereby causing you trouble

singularities Rarities

lively In life-like fashion

Hermione was ... seems A true touch, which brings home the passage of time

So many summers dry Nor which sixteen summers can dry up

him ... this Polixenes means himself

take ... himself i.e. share your grief until he bears as much as you (and therefore halves yours). For 'piece' see note p.80.

wrought Affected

already— Leontes breaks off and leaves his sentence unfinished.

fixture Fixed (immovable) state

settled i.e. same

On i.e. let what I am about to do go on

upon On

double A second time

pertain to life Live

Like an old tale The words of the Third Gentleman in Scene 2

interpose Come in front of her, come between her and the others. Paulina is speaking to Perdita.

vials Flasks

push Impulse

winners People who have got what you wanted

Partake to Share with
lost Dead
consent Agreement
Is ... justified Are highly reputed and here testified
whom Strictly speaking should be 'who'
troth plight Betrothed to marry
demand ... dissever'd Ask and answer questions about the part
  he has played in this wide interval of time, since first we were
  separated

Revision Questions on Act V

1 Contrast Leontes' fairness in suspending judgement on
Florizel until he has heard both sides with his impetuous condemnation of Hermione earlier in the play.

2 Give an account of important events in this Act which are
not shown on the stage.

3 Give a full account of the scene where the statue comes to
life as Hermione herself.

4 Do you feel satisfied by the marriage arranged for Paulina?
Give your reasons.

General questions

1 Give a brief account of the plot of *The Winter's Tale*.

2 Discuss the part played in the plot by Camillo and Antigonus. What is your opinion of the introduction of a bear to dispose of Antigonus?

3 Which features of the play are too improbable for you to believe in?

4 Why is *The Winter's Tale* classed as one of Shakespeare's 'Romances'?

5 '*The Winter's Tale* is, as its title suggests, a tale for the fireside rather than a picture of life' (p.6). Discuss this.

6 Had you not been told, how could you judge that *The Winter's Tale* was among the last of Shakespeare's plays?

7 Describe Shakespeare's picture of rustic life in the play and, if you are able, compare it with the picture in *As You Like It* or *Cymbeline*.

8 What *dramatic* purposes are served by the sheep-shearing feast?

9 Lytton Strachey says that Shakespeare was 'half bored to death' writing *The Winter's Tale*. Does the character of Leontes offer any evidence for this?

10 Mention an occasion when you feel some sympathy for Leontes.

11 Compare and contrast the characters of Leontes and Polixenes.

12 What light is thrown on the characters of (a) Leontes, (b) Hermione, (c) Perdita by other people's remarks about them?

13 By reference to any two characters, illustrate Shakespeare's power of depicting women.

14 Give examples of (a) the self-control of Hermione, (b) the impulsiveness of Paulina, (c) the roguery of Autolycus.

15 'Really, Autolycus is independent of the main action of the plot.' (p.23) Do you think that the play would suffer if the Autolycus episodes were omitted?

16 Give an estimate of Shakespeare's sense of humour, as illustrated by the figures of Autolycus and the Clown.

17 'All the important characters of *The Winter's Tale* are deceitful at some point, with good or bad intent' (p.24). Give examples.

18 What characteristic features of Shakespeare's dramatic art are to be found in (a) the scene of Hermione's trial, (b) the great pastoral scene?

19 Quote any beautiful passages of poetry which add to your enjoyment of the play, with a few critical comments.

20 Give an instance from the play of (a) simile, (b) metaphor, (c) antithesis, (d) paradox, (e) personification, (f) dramatic irony.

21 Mention at least three places in the play where prose is the medium and suggest reasons for its use in each case.

22 Describe an imaginary visit to an Elizabethan theatre for a performance of *The Winter's Tale*.

23 By what means has the text of Shakespeare's plays been determined?

Pan study aids Titles published in the Brodie's Notes series

W. H. Auden Selected Poetry

Jane Austen Emma Mansfield Park Northanger Abbey Persuasion
Pride and Prejudice

Anthologies of Poetry Ten Twentieth Century Poets
The Metaphysical Poets The Poet's Tale

Samuel Beckett Waiting for Godot

Arnold Bennett The Old Wives' Tale

William Blake Songs of Innocence and Experience

Robert Bolt A Man for All Seasons

Harold Brighouse Hobson's Choice

Charlotte Brontë Jane Eyre

Emily Brontë Wuthering Heights

Robert Browning Selected Poetry

John Bunyan The Pilgrim's Progress

Geoffrey Chaucer (parallel texts editions) The Franklin's Tale
The Knight's Tale The Miller's Tale The Nun's Priest's Tale
The Pardoner's Tale Prologue to the Canterbury Tales
The Wife of Bath's Tale

Richard Church Over the Bridge

John Clare Selected Poetry and Prose

Samuel Taylor Coleridge Selected Poetry and Prose

Wilkie Collins The Woman in White

William Congreve The Way of the World

Joseph Conrad The Nigger of the Narcissus & Youth
The Secret Agent

Charles Dickens Bleak House David Copperfield Dombey and Son
Great Expectations Hard Times Little Dorrit Oliver Twist
Our Mutual Friend A Tale of Two Cities

Gerald Durrell My Family and Other Animals

George Eliot Middlemarch The Mill on the Floss Silas Marner

T. S. Eliot Murder in the Cathedral Selected Poems

J. G. Farrell The Siege of Krishnapur

Henry Fielding Joseph Andrews

F. Scott Fitzgerald The Great Gatsby